BLESSED

David Cerullo

BLESSED

Inspiration Ministries
P.O. Box 7750
Charlotte, NC 28241 USA

ISBN Number: 978-1-936177-03-5

TABLE *of* CONTENTS

BLESSED

INTRODUCTION

*"Let us hold fast the confession of our hope
without wavering, for He who promised is faithful."*
—HEBREWS 10:23

My friend, do you need a miracle? Have you tried everything? Have you looked everywhere? You may feel like all hell has broken loose in your life and that it's impossible for things to change.

Know today the devil is not in control. All stress, poverty, depression, loneliness, anxiety, sickness, and lack are rooted in the enemy trying to exercise his power and authority over you and your circumstances. But God has a plan and a purpose for you. He is able to set you FREE!

You may be thinking, "It would take a miracle to set me free from my problems!" This is exactly what God wants to give you. His blessings are for you NOW. And that's why I've written this book. If you're looking for hope when it feels like all hope is gone, and you need…

    ❧ Answers to a desperate situation
    ❧ Freedom from financial debt
    ❧ God's healing power in your body
    ❧ A pain-filled relationship restored
    ❧ A more intimate relationship with the Lord

...then know you haven't picked up this book today by accident. My prayer is that as you read through these pages, your heart will be completely open to what only God can do for you through His love and power.

Your Breakthrough Is Coming!

Scripture says that after God delivered King David from his enemy, he testified, *"The LORD has broken through my enemies before me, like a breakthrough of water"* (2 Samuel 5:20).

I have good news for you today: Just as God moved in the midst of David's desperate circumstances, He has a breakthrough on His mind for you. God is a good God, and He loves you beyond your ability to comprehend it. And because of the depth of His love for you, He wants to bless you.

> *Blessed is the man who trusts in him...those who seek the LORD shall not lack any good thing.*
>
> PSALM 34:8–10

The Bible says, *"Oh taste and see that the LORD is good; blessed is the man who trusts in him...those who seek the LORD shall not lack any good thing"* (Psalm 34:8–10).

If you're going through anxious times, God wants you to turn to Him to be your Provider. He is your Source. He wants to free you from fear and worry. He wants you to depend on Him, not on your job, your relationships, your bank account, your pastor, the government, or your own strength. Regardless of the anxious, painful, or difficult situation you may be experiencing today, know that God wants to prosper you: *"Let the*

INTRODUCTION

LORD *be magnified, Who has pleasure in the prosperity of His servant"* (Psalm 35:27).

God doesn't want you to suffer lack. He intends for you to have more than enough. More than enough energy. More than enough time. More than enough joy for living. And more than enough financial resources so that you can give to others out of the abundance of what He has given you.

He says in His Word, *"Beloved, I pray that you may prosper in all things and be in health, just as your soul prospers"* (3 John 2). But sadly, too many Christians are experiencing life at a level way BELOW the blessings God has planned for them:

❧ Many are living in the land of "Not Enough."
❧ Others are living in the land of "Just Enough."
❧ Very few are living in the land of **"More Than Enough!"**

Wouldn't it be so much better if receiving God's continuous blessings were a way of life? What peace, joy, and security we could know if only we would walk with Him hand-in-hand like obedient, hopeful children, confident that our every need will be provided for as we trust in the faithfulness of our loving Heavenly Father.

God Is Able!

When we were little children, we learned simple, basic math. Well, in this book, I give you a "spiritual equation"—one so easy, so simple, that if you will choose to follow this equation faithfully

BLESSED
INTRODUCTION

and put it into practice immediately, God will begin to release His Harvests of Blessings in your life.

Not only that, but I also share with you 12 powerful, Biblically based "Blessing Keys" that will unleash His joy and fill your life so full that it's overflowing with His abundant blessings.

God's desire is to transform your circumstances, your health, your relationships, your finances, and your spirit. His intention is to lead you into a place of abundant life that only He can give. His goal is to pour out His blessings over you in a new and wonderful way.

Be filled with hope. Your life will never ever be the same as you allow God to change your mind, change your heart, and change your life.

God Bless You,

David

BLESSED

*Knowing that
you were called
to this, that
you may inherit
a blessing.*

1 PETER 3:9

1 Blessed to Be a Blessing

Barbara and I have received literally thousands of prayer requests from people struggling in the midst of painful situations.

They've lost their jobs, and they've lost their homes. Marriages are crumbling, and children are rebelling. They're struggling to overcome addiction, and they're overwhelmed by depression. Their bodies are aching, and their spirits are suffering. They long for God to move in their life, but they feel hopeless. They desperately need a breakthrough, but they doubt His love and His desire to intervene in the midst of their circumstances. My heart breaks for them. Read just a few of their desperate situations…

"Please pray for me and my wife. We're at the edge of a separation, and I fear our hearts are hardened. I pray for God's will to be done, but there are so many unresolved issues. I love her so much." —James

"I am depressed. I can't talk to anyone about it. Only God can make it go away. The anger is relentless, and the feeling of hopelessness is choking the life out of me. I feel as if my sadness and sins make me unworthy to even call on His name. Please pray for me." —Carla

"My husband needs to be delivered from alcohol. He has been drinking for many years and has violent outbursts that scare our children. I am seriously thinking about leaving because he always lies about stopping. He also has turned away from God for about six years. I'm at the end now, and I am feeling that there's no other way for me. I know God can deliver him. I just don't know if He will. Please pray for me and my husband." —Paula

"I have been laid off from my job of 11 years, and I am the sole provider of my family. I will lose my home and vehicles. I need God to help me. I feel I am living a nightmare right now, and I just want to give up." —Hector

"Please pray for me and my family. I want a stronger walk with Jesus. I want to know more about Him and get closer to Him. My family needs to be saved. I am the only one who is saved right now, so I need prayer that God can use me to be a light to them." —Jessica

"My heart is breaking. I want peace, love, and joy to come. I feel so alone." —Tamie

As my wife Barbara and I pray over their needs, we feel their pain. In my heart of hearts, I know God wants to break through in their circumstances. He wants to do miracles in their lives. He wants to heal them. He wants to give them His joy and abundant provision. God's heart is to bless His children.

Perhaps you can identify with some of these precious ones who have written to ask us for prayer. I know I can. Through the years, Barbara and I have experienced some painful and challenging times—times when the only thing that would help was a miracle, and we sure couldn't see a miracle coming.

I can remember as if it were yesterday when we broke open our son's piggy bank just so we could go get a burger to split for our dinner. I was out of work, and we were broke. I didn't know how I was going to pay the car loan, make the mortgage payment, or put food on the table. It's a terrible thing to feel like you can't provide for your family. I had a wife and a baby, and I was desperate. But God came through for us in a mighty and powerful way: He blessed me with a consulting job that paid thousands of dollars for a day's work, and then I in turn was able to bless my family and others as I gave out of what He had given me.

> *Stop for a minute and get a hold of this truth: God is saying to YOU, "I will bless YOU...and YOU shall be a blessing."*

Know today that God wants to move in powerful ways to overcome the circumstances of your life. He is the God of the entire universe, and He has promised to bless you.

God's Covenant Blessings Are for YOU

Here is one of God's exceedingly great and precious promises to you: *"I will bless you...and you shall be a blessing"* (Genesis 12:2). Stop for a minute and get a hold of this truth: God is saying to *YOU, "I will bless YOU...and YOU shall be a blessing."*

Now, perhaps you're thinking, "Wait a minute Dave. I know that Bible story, and God was talking to Abraham—not me—when He made that promise." Well, that's true. But according to Galatians 3, the promises God made to Abraham, He also made to us. This Scripture passage says that Abraham...

...believed God, and it was accounted to him for righteousness. Therefore know that only those who are of faith are sons of Abraham...that the blessing of Abraham might come upon the Gentiles in Christ Jesus, that we might receive the promise of the Spirit through faith... Now to Abraham and his Seed were the promises made (vs. 6–16).

Do you see? Abraham's promises are our promises. If you're a Believer today...if Jesus Christ is your Lord and Savior...then you, too, are Abraham's seed, and the blessings and promises of Abraham are yours. And like Abraham, as you receive God's blessings, you can be a blessing to others!

> *Don't let past disappointments cause you to turn away from your God-given destiny.*

The promise that God made to Abraham—and to you—was a **Covenant**. God made this Covenant with him because He wanted to have a relationship with Abraham. Let me give you a great example to help you understand the concept of Covenant Relationship...

On our wedding day, Barbara and I exchanged vows. We made promises to each other to love and cherish one another for the rest of our lives. Ours was a love relationship sealed by the covenant we made with one another before God and all our wedding guests. This is the kind of love relationship the Lord wants to have with us. He loves us so much that He wants us to live in a Covenant Relationship with Him forever.

A Covenant is a solemn, binding agreement between two parties. To covenant with someone means that those involved will stand behind their word, no matter what. Just like Barbara and I made a covenant promise to be faithful to one another as husband and wife until the day we die, God has made Covenant Promises to us.

Here is a powerful truth you must grab hold of deep in your spirit: *God is a God of Covenants.* He can't and won't forget them. He will stand behind His Word every time, and He will never be unfaithful to what He has covenanted with us to do.

The Lord is stirring such compassion in my heart for you right now. You want to believe this truth is for you. You want to believe it's this simple. You want to trust that what the Bible says about God's Covenant Blessings is true, but perhaps you're afraid. Maybe you've been waiting a long time for God to pour out His blessings in your life, but you're tired of waiting.

If this describes where you are today, then know that God understands. He sees your heart. He knows your need. He has compassion for your brokenness. You're not reading this book today by accident. He wants to break through in the midst of your circumstances and release His Covenant Blessings in your life—to bless you, and then equip you to be a blessing to others.

Don't let past disappointments cause you to turn away from your God-given destiny, your calling in Christ, your mission in life. I said it before, and I'll say it again: God's promise to you from Genesis 12:2 is true: *"I will bless you…and you shall be a blessing."* Today can be the beginning of a breakthrough in your life.

Jesus Wants to Climb in Your "Boat"

I believe the Lord wants to intervene in everyone's circumstances. He is willing and ready to release His breakthroughs over all who have prepared their hearts to receive Him. But the sad truth is that not everyone prepares their hearts for Him. As a result, so many of us aren't walking in the reality of His Covenant Blessings that we so desperately need. Let me tell you a story to encourage you to prepare your heart to receive all He has planned for you.

One stormy and windy night, Jesus' disciples were in a boat out on the sea. They were weary from straining to row the boat to shore, and their situation was desperate. Mark 6:48 (NASB) says that Jesus *"came to them, walking on the sea; and He intended to pass by them."* The disciples cried out in fear, thinking they were seeing a ghost. But this story has such a great ending. When the disciples finally recognized Jesus, He assured them, *"Take courage; it is I. Do not be afraid"* (v. 50). Then He climbed into the boat with them, and the wind stopped.

My friend, this is exactly what Jesus wants to do in your life today. He wants to get into your "boat" with you—right there in the midst of your storms and difficult circumstances. He wants to speak a powerful word over your troubling situations, stilling the winds of adversity that the enemy has brought your way. The devil will do everything he can to stop, thwart, or hinder God's plan for your health, your relationships, and your finances. That's his agenda. Jesus warns us in John 10:10 (NASB) that *"the thief comes only to steal and kill and destroy."*

But then He goes on to say, *"I came that they may have life, and have it abundantly."* Jesus has come to give you an abundant life! Jesus wants to climb into your boat today, right now.

He loves you and is able AND willing to intervene as you prepare your heart to receive His Covenant Blessings in your life. *"Blessed be the God and Father of our Lord Jesus Christ, who has blessed us with every spiritual blessing in the heavenly places in Christ"*

(Ephesians 1:3). Then as you receive God's blessings, you will be equipped and empowered to bless others:

Here Is Your 1st Harvest Key:

YOU ARE BLESSED TO BE A BLESSING!

Let me pray for you...

> *Heavenly Father, thank You that You are a Covenant-Making, Covenant-Keeping God. Thank You that Your heart's desire is to release Your Covenant Blessings over Your precious child. I ask today that You would prepare their heart to receive all You have in store for them, to prosper them, bless them, and to make them a blessing. I pray this in Jesus' Name. Amen.*

Now be encouraged by this testimony of how God blessed Sherry and how she is now a blessing to others because of His amazing intervention in her life!

'You Will Not Commit Suicide!'

"After years of marriage to an unsaved alcoholic, at age 34 I finally left my husband. Brokenhearted and attempting to escape my pain, I became an alcoholic myself. For 16 years, I struggled with addictions and toxic relationships with men. I destroyed my relationships with my mother and children, and I was physically malnourished and spiritually empty.

"One day I called in sick to work, took my last diet pill, and grabbed a knife to slash my wrists and end my life. But at this moment of overwhelming emotional pain, I cried out in desperation, 'God, please help me if You can!'

I'm now free from addictions, and God has restored my health and my relationships with my mother and children!

"Suddenly, I heard a voice coming from one of your television broadcasts—though I hadn't even been aware the TV was on. Amazingly, the speaker said, 'You will not kill yourself today!' I sat straight up in bed, and the buzzing high from the amphetamine pill quickly evaporated, making it possible for me to focus my attention on the minister preaching on the screen. Seeming to point directly at me, he said again, 'You will not commit suicide today, because you are a precious child of the Most High God!'

Recognizing this word was for me, I responded, 'I choose to live!' Then I prayed the most direct prayer to our Heavenly Father that I'd prayed in a long while. I asked the Lord, 'If You want me to live, how can I face all the struggles and addictions in my life?' God gently replied, 'I will be with you.'

"The Lord has indeed walked with me since then. As a result, I watch your network every day, and I'm so grateful for the impact you and your Inspiration Partners have had on my life. Now the Lord is leading me to Sow back into the Good Ground of your ministry. As God has blessed me, I want to be a blessing to others, so enclosed is my monthly $58 Seed, based on Isaiah 58!" — **Sherry**

My friend, what God has done for Sherry, He can do for *you!*

BLESSED

*But without faith
it is impossible to
please Him, for he
who comes to God
must believe that
He is, and that He
is a rewarder of
those who diligently
seek Him.*

HEBREWS 11:6

A Harvest Equation

In the Introduction of this book, I told you I would share a simple Scriptural equation with you that will release the treasures of Heaven in your life, and here it is:

FAITH + OBEDIENCE + EXPECTANCY = GOD'S UNCOMMON HARVEST

So what does this equation mean? Let me explain…

There have been many times when Barbara and I had to have the **faith** that God wanted to—and that He would—move powerfully on our behalf. We **obeyed** whatever He told us to do, and we **expected** God to bless us with His love and power.

I remember one time in particular when our son Ben was an infant. He was burning up with a 104.5-degree fever. We called our pediatrician, who told us to bring Ben to the emergency room right away. He didn't say to bring him to his office, but to go immediately to the emergency room at the hospital. We knew it was serious!

Barbara and I were rushing out the door when I sensed the Holy Spirit's leading. I stopped and said to her, "Before we go, let's pray and anoint him with oil, and see what God will do." We sat down together on the couch with Ben in our arms. As we anointed him with oil, we laid hands on him and prayed the Prayer of Faith together.

While we were praying, our little baby boy literally went from burning up with fever to being completely cool, with no fever and a perfectly normal temperature. There was no need for us to take him to the emergency room. For two young parents with their first child, this was an amazing, miraculous breakthrough. As we exercised our FAITH + OBEDIENCE + EXPECTANCY, God blessed us.

Faith is the belief that God will intervene in our circumstances, knowing that if we love God, we are called according to His purpose and He causes all things to work together for our good (Romans 8:28).

As we exercised our FAITH + OBEDIENCE + EXPECTANCY, God blessed us.

Obedience means putting our faith into action, which happens when we 1) read His Word and follow what it says, and 2) listen to the voice of His Holy Spirit and obey what He tells us to do. Jesus tells us, *"You are My friends if you do whatever I command you"* (John 15:14).

Expectancy is a sense of hope-filled waiting that only comes after we've prayed in faith, believing that God will intervene in our circumstances, and then are obedient to His Word and His Holy Spirit. We must wrap our faith and obedience with expectation and then trust Him to be faithful to His Covenant Promises.

In Lamentations 3:22–26 (NASB), the prophet Jeremiah speaks these comforting and encouraging words to us:

The LORD'S lovingkindnesses indeed never cease,
for His compassions never fail. They are new every
morning; great is Your faithfulness. "The LORD is my
portion," says my soul, "Therefore I have hope in Him."
The LORD is good to those who **wait** *for Him, to the*
person who seeks Him. It is good that he **waits** *silently*
for the salvation of the LORD.

The word "wait" used in this passage is from the Hebrew word *qavah,* which means to wait with hope and expectancy.

Numbers 23:19 (NASB) clearly tells us, *"God is not a man, that He should lie, nor a son of man, that He should repent; has He said, and will He not do it? Or has He spoken, and will He not make it good?"*

You can trust that God is who He says He is and that He will do what He says He will do. He promises to watch over His Word to perform it (Jeremiah 1:12).

There are many Biblical examples of people in desperate situations who applied FAITH + OBEDIENCE + EXPECTANCY, and God intervened with His Harvests in amazing ways in their lives. There's Jairus, who had faith, obeyed, and expected Jesus to move on behalf of his daughter, and He raised her from the dead!

Then there's the mother whose daughter was demon possessed. She, too, had faith and obeyed with expectancy, and Jesus set her daughter free! Or how about the woman who had been bleeding for 12 years? The doctors couldn't help her, so she went to Jesus for help. Her actions were based on FAITH + OBEDIENCE + EXPECTANCY, which resulted in her healing and Jesus saying to her, "Your faith has made you whole."

In order for God to release His Covenant Blessings in our lives, He requires us to apply FAITH + OBEDIENCE + EXPECTANCY in every circumstance. We believe in God's Covenant Promises, we obey whatever He asks us to do, and then we wait with expectation for Him to stand behind His Word and fulfill His Covenant Promises to us. This is one of the primary ways we show our love for Him.

Seedtime and Harvest

In Chapter 1, I shared with you the powerful Covenant God made with Abraham— and with us—to bless us and to make us a blessing. Well, before He made that Covenant with Abraham, He made another eternal and unchanging Covenant with us—one that will powerfully impact your life and circumstances right now if you will choose to live by it.

The first recorded Covenant in Scripture is found in Genesis, where we learn in Chapter 6 that Noah was *"a just man, perfect in his generations"* and that he *"walked with God"* (v. 9). Because of Noah's faithfulness and obedience, God saved him and his family from the destruction of the flood that ended all other life on earth. He promised Noah, *"I will establish My Covenant with you"* (v. 18).

As soon as the land was dry, the first thing Noah did was to honor God by building Him an altar, and giving an offering…a sacrifice…to Him. God's heart was touched by Noah's actions, and He responded by making this Covenant with him: *"While the earth remains, seedtime and harvest, cold and heat, winter and summer, and day and night shall not cease"* (Genesis 8:22).

Isn't it amazing that the first recorded Covenant in Scripture also contains God's eternal principle of Seedtime and Harvest?

When you chose to respond to God's love by inviting Jesus Christ to be your Lord, you entered into a Covenant with Him, and ALL the blessings of Scripture became yours.(Galatians 3:6–14) The same Covenant God made with Noah is still in effect for you today!

Now, remember that a covenant is an agreement between two parties, like the wedding vows Barbara and I made on our wedding day. In order for our covenant with one another to remain unbroken, both of us must remain faithful to our marriage vows. In the same way, God has established His unending Seedtime and Harvest Covenant with us because He loves us. He will never fail to fulfill what He has promised to do.

"While the earth remains, seedtime and harvest, shall not cease" (Genesis 8:22).

But what does God require of us in this Covenant Relationship? **Faith, obedience,** and **expectancy** are all "Seeds" God asks us to Sow into His Kingdom. And what is it He promises we will Reap from these spiritual Seeds? His Harvest of Blessings!

If you will allow God's Holy Spirit to impart this truth deep in your spirit, then your life…your circumstances…your struggles…can start to turn around TODAY!

I've traveled all over the world and prayed for thousands of Believers. What I've observed is that too many of us are experiencing life at a level WAY below the blessings God intends for us to experience. All too often we just live our lives until we experience a crisis: We lose our job…our finances are depleted…our spouse leaves us…our child becomes addicted to drugs…we get sick. We become caught up in a cycle of defeat, depression, and despair…and then we cry out to God in desperation for Him to bless us.

What would life be like if we just chose to live in an unending cycle of God's blessing as a way of life? This is the kind of Covenant Living God wants us to experience. He has promised us that Seedtime and Harvest shall not cease. And with God, a promise is a promise is a promise. If we will take Him at His Word and stand on His Covenant Promises by simply having faith, obeying Him, and then expecting Him to move on our behalf, we will have discovered a vital key to living in His joy and receiving His blessings.

The simple, yet profound, truth is this: **God wants a relationship with us.** That's why He sent His Son to die on the Cross. Jesus was a Seed God planted on the earth so that He could Reap an eternal Harvest of sons and daughters.

Jesus knew this. He said to His disciples, *"Unless a grain of wheat falls into the ground and dies, it remains alone; but if it dies, it produces much grain"* (John 12:24). Jesus was talking about Himself, and He became living, eternal proof that Seedtime and Harvest shall NEVER cease! If Jesus is our Lord and Savior, then all of God's Covenants and Promises are ours.

It's so simple, really. God loves us. We love Him back. And we show our love for Him when we live for Him, have faith, obey Him, and expect Him to do what He has promised to do. God then responds by giving us His joy and pouring out His Blessings over our lives. He blesses us, not just for our own sake, but so that we can be a blessing to others. We give back to Him, and He gives us more. This is His unending cycle of Covenant Relationship that He invites us to continually experience.

Obey God in Small AND in Big Ways

From the thousands of amazing testimonies Barbara and I receive here at Inspiration Ministries each month, I know that so many of our partners are walking in a loving, obedient Covenant Relationship with God…spending time with Him in prayer, worshipping Him, and reading the Scriptures as they faithfully Sow Seeds, obey His Word and the leading of His Holy Spirit, and wait expectantly to Reap His Harvests.

But sadly, we also receive letters from many who are neglecting their relationship with Him. Some are even openly living in sin while still asking God to reward their wrong choices with His blessings. Then they don't understand why they aren't Reaping His Uncommon Harvests in their lives. They don't realize that their sin separates them from God. If they want to Reap His Blessings, they must consistently live in a loving, faith-filled, obedient relationship with Him.

God wants us to walk in a continuous, loving Covenant Relationship with Him, faithfully choosing to obey Him and then waiting expectantly for Him to move in our situation. As we do, He promises...

> *Now it shall be, if you diligently obey the Lord your God, being careful to do all His commandments which I command you today, that the LORD will set you high above all the nations of the earth.* ***And all these blessings will come upon you and overtake you*** (Deuteronomy 28:1–2).

Most of us are obedient to God in the "big" things—we don't murder anyone, we don't have an affair with our neighbor's spouse, we don't commit armed bank robbery. But all too often, we're disobedient in "small" ways: we're unkind and disrespectful to loved ones or strangers, we watch a lust-filled TV program, we gossip, we don't return the extra change we receive in the checkout line...

But God wants us to obey Him in both the big AND the small things. When we do, we will see Him move on our behalf.

My friend, faithfully obey whatever God is calling you to do. You can trust Him to help and strengthen you because He loves you. He is your loving Heavenly Father, and you are His child. Know that every act of obedience lessens the distance between you and the Harvest you're waiting for God to supply!

Know that every act of obedience lessens the distant between you and the Harvest you're waiting for God to supply!

His principle of Seedtime and Harvest is eternal, and you can stand on His promises. As you faithfully and obediently walk in a Covenant Relationship with Him, you can have great expectations for your future and be hope-filled about the plans God has for you!

Here Is Your 2nd Harvest Key:

FAITH + OBEDIENCE + EXPECTANCY = GOD'S HARVEST OF BLESSINGS IN YOUR LIFE!

Let me pray for you…

Heavenly Father, thank You for Your goodness and faithfulness to us, and thank You for establishing your Covenant of Seedtime and Harvest. Please move in your child's heart and mind. Fill them with faith and the courage to obey, and cause hope to rise up within them as they expectantly wait on You to meet their every need and release your Covenant Blessings in their life. I pray this in Jesus' Name. Amen.

Now be encouraged by this testimony of how God blessed William and his family because they believed God, obeyed Him, and waited expectantly for Him to release His Harvest of Blessings over their desperate situation!

'I Believed God with Great Expectation'

"Last year, my mother-in-law, Natalina, who was 93, suddenly took ill. When my wife Mary and her sister were able to get to the hospital, they found her semiconscious with a severe case of pneumonia due to choking on some food.

"Doctors explained the severity of the situation, saying that if Natalina did regain full consciousness, it would just be a matter of time before she passed. Because her aorta was only the size of a soda straw, her organs weren't getting the proper supply of blood needed to sustain life. She wouldn't be able to swallow because of paralysis in her throat. In addition, she most likely would have repeated episodes of this crisis on a regular basis. They recommended putting her on a morphine drip and letting her go peacefully.

"Around this same time, I received an email from Inspiration Ministries stating that whatever we prayed for, God could do, if we really believed. So I Sowed a Seed and requested prayer for my wonderful mother-in-law's healing. Then I truly believed and expected God to faithfully answer.

"The day after I sent my Seed and prayer request, Mary went to the hospital to visit her mother again. But she nearly fainted when she saw her. Amazingly, Natalina was sitting up in a chair, even though she had been hospitalized and near death for more than a week!

I just had to share this testament of His faithfulness that we witnessed after I stepped out in faith and believed God with great expectation.

"Her doctors were astonished at her remarkable recovery too. But they inserted a stomach tube to feed her, which they said she would need to have for the rest of her life. She wouldn't be able to eat solid food again. Then they sent her to a nursing home to recuperate for three weeks.

"One night after she had come home, Natalina woke up, and to our horror pulled the stomach tube out, declaring that she had just seen Jesus, and He had told her she no longer needed it!

Alarmed, we called the nurse at 2:00 a.m. She came and reinserted the feeding tube, only to have Natalina pull it out again a day or two later as she adamantly exclaimed, 'I told you all I don't need this anymore. Jesus told me I don't need this tube anymore!'

"Ever since that day more than a year ago, my mother-in-law has been able to eat anything and everything she wants—including bowls of pasta, which she loves. We are constantly amazed by her hearty appetite and how happy, content, full of wit, mental sharpness, and mobility she is, especially since she is almost 94.

"I just had to let you all know about this wonderful miracle of God and share this testament of His faithfulness that we witnessed after I stepped out in faith and **believed God with great expectation."** — **William**

My friend, what God has done for William, He can do for *you!*

BLESSED

He turns a wilderness into pools of water, and dry land into watersprings. There He makes the hungry dwell, that they may establish a city for a dwelling place, and sow fields and plant vineyards that they may yield a fruitful harvest. He also blesses them, and they multiply greatly...

PSALM 107:35-38a

In the Beginning

 S eeds are pretty amazing, aren't they? Inside each one, God has deposited specific DNA to determine what that seed will become. Every seed that a farmer plants in good soil and carefully tends is destined to yield a fruitful harvest.

When you think about, it's clear that everything begins with a seed...

 ❧ An apple orchard began with an apple seed.
 ❧ Amazing inventions like the computer began with the seed of an idea.
 ❧ Disneyland began with the seed of a vision.
 ❧ A thousand dollars saved began with a seed of a dollar.
 ❧ Jesus' life on earth began with the seed of the Holy Spirit.
 ❧ Even *your* life began as tiny, microscopic seed!

As I shared with you in the previous chapter, the first Covenant God established with Noah—and with us—was His eternal principle of Seedtime and Harvest. So it makes sense that everything begins with a seed.

In the natural, it's easy to understand the principle of sowing seeds and reaping a harvest. A farmer plants seeds, ensures that they receive plenty of sun and rain and that the soil is healthy and well fertilized. As he diligently tends his seeds, they produce a healthy and life-sustaining harvest.

Well, what's true in the natural regarding seedtime and harvest is also true in the spiritual. As you Sow Seeds into Good Ground and are diligent to fertilize them with your faith, obedience, and expectancy, you will Reap a life-sustaining, God-given Harvest for your good and His glory. But when times are hard, it's easy to get discouraged and become focused on what you don't have rather than what you do have.

Do you ever find yourself thinking, "I would love to give, but I barely have enough for my own needs," or "I'm just too tired to help," or "As soon as I have more time, I'll serve the Lord," or "If only I had more faith, I would pray more for others."

Most people who are living in the lands of "Not Enough" or "Just Enough" are taking inventory of their NEEDS…what they don't have…or what they wished they had. If you truly want to live in God's Promised Land of "More Than Enough," then it's time for you to take inventory of your SEEDS…what you do have!

What is a Seed? A Seed is anything you've received from God that you can give back to God for Him to multiply. You are a walking warehouse of Seeds! Here is a list of Seeds you can Sow into His Kingdom:

❦ Love	❦ Patience	❦ Money	❦ Thoughts	❦ Talents
❦ Forgiveness	❦ Time	❦ Kindness	❦ Prayer	❦ Joy
❦ Gratitude	❦ Hope	❦ Faith	❦ Humor	❦ Help

So let me ask you right now: What God-Given Seeds do you have to Sow that can Reap a Harvest? Instead of concentrating on your NEEDS, I challenge you to inventory your SEEDS. Then start Sowing them into Good Ground! Your Seed is the...

 ❧ Exit from your present!
 ❧ Door to your future!
 ❧ Bridge leading you out of the lands of "Not Enough" or "Just Enough" to a land of *"More Than Enough"* filled with God's Uncommon Harvests!

If you truly want to live in God's Promised Land of "More Than Enough," then it's time for you to take inventory of your SEEDS... what you do have!

Remember: Everything begins with a Seed. Do you need a Harvest in some area of your life? Don't withhold your Seed because of your need. Sow your Seed because of your need. Stop focusing on what you DON'T have; instead, concentrate on what you DO have, and then Sow them as Seeds into God's Kingdom. When you do, then you can expect to Reap God's Covenant Blessings in your life.

Uncommon Seeds, Uncommon Harvests

When something is uncommon, it's unusual...different. An "Uncommon Seed" is an out-of-the-ordinary Seed. It's a Seed you probably wouldn't normally Sow. It's above and beyond what you would typically give.

 ❧ A Seed's *size* can make it UNCOMMON.
 ❧ A Seed that requires great *sacrifice* is UNCOMMON.
 ❧ A Seed Sown in faith-filled *obedience* is UNCOMMON.
 ❧ A Seed Sown during a time of *crisis* is UNCOMMON.

When you Sow an Uncommon Seed into God's Kingdom, it

becomes magnified in His eyes. That's why an Uncommon Seed always produces an "Uncommon Harvest."

So what makes a Harvest Blessing from God Uncommon?

❧ A Harvest's *size* can make it UNCOMMON.
❧ A Harvest that is clearly the result of an Uncommon Seed is UNCOMMON.
❧ A Harvest that comes from an unexpected source is UNCOMMON.
❧ A Harvest that you couldn't produce on your own is UNCOMMON.

Why does God want you to Sow Uncommon Seeds and Reap His Uncommon Harvests? Because He loves you! Because He wants you to live continuously in the cycle of His of Seedtime and Harvest principle! Because He wants to bless you and make you a blessing to others!

A good friend of mine likes to say, "If you want something you've never had, you have to do something you've never done." Something out of the ordinary...something uncommon.

Remember, *"Seedtime and harvest...shall not cease."* God is a God of Covenants. He stands behind His Word. He will not be—He cannot be—unfaithful to what He has Covenanted with His people to do. God loves it when we believe Him and all the promises in His Word. We can trust Him to ALWAYS produce Uncommon Harvests from our Uncommon Seeds.

An Uncommon Number: 58

Through the years, lots of people have come up with different numbers for how many blessings are contained in Scripture, but the number I believe is most accurate is 58. There may be more or there may be less, but that's how many I count. And 58 blessings is a lot of blessings!

God promises that these blessings are yours…if you will be obedient to what He asks in this Scripture passage: Set the prisoner free, feed the hungry, take care of the poor, and reach out with His compassion to afflicted Souls.

There are 58 blessings throughout God's Word.

Barbara and I have received multiplied thousands of testimonies from people who have chosen to believe God, obey what His Holy Spirit was leading them to do, and then waited with expectancy. And as they partnered with Inspiration Ministries by Sowing an Uncommon *$58* Seed each month to bring the love and hope of Jesus Christ into more than 120 nations…and touch more than 1.2 billion people worldwide…God has released these four miracles in their lives and blessed their faith, obedience, and expectation with His Uncommon Harvests!

You see, when we get involved with God's dream, God gets involved with our dream.

Sixty thousand children have written this ministry to let us know they've been impacted by our kids programming, which is created because of the prayers and financial Seeds Sown into God's Kingdom through the Good Ground of this ministry. If I get involved with somebody else's child, God gets involved with mine.

Thousands of teens have been saved and their lives transformed because of our ministry to young people. Again, this is made possible by those who pray and Sow Seed into the Kingdom of God through the outreaches of Inspiration Ministries. What we make happen for somebody else's teen, God can make happen for our teen.

> *As you are faithful to honor Him with thankful hearts, He will be faithful to honor you with even more blessings in return!*

Every month, our international prayer ministry prays with literally thousands of people over the phone. The sick are getting healed. People enslaved by debt are being set free. Marriages are being restored. Do you see? As God blesses you, you Sow Seed to bless others. Then what you have done to bless others, He will do for you. You receive His Uncommon Harvest Blessings in your body…your finances…your marriage…your life. And then He gives you more Seed to Sow!

Seven Steps to Receiving Your UNCOMMON Harvest

How can you ensure that your Uncommon Seeds will produce God's Uncommon Harvests in your life? Just faithfully follow these seven steps:

1. Walk in a loving, obedient Covenant Relationship with God.
2. Obey God's Word and the voice of His Holy Spirit.
3. Sow your Uncommon Seed into Good Ground. (More about this in Chapter 6!)
4. Sow your Uncommon Seed faithfully.
5. Wrap your Uncommon Seed with expectancy.
6. Wait patiently to Reap your Uncommon Harvest.
7. Honor God with your testimony of His Uncommon Harvests in your life!

Keep in mind that Step 6 is just as important as Steps 1–5! Remember that it was after the flood that Noah built an altar to honor God and thank Him for His faithfulness, and *then* God made His Covenant. When you testify to others of how God has blessed you with His Uncommon Harvests, you are building an "altar" in your heart to honor and thank Him for His faithfulness. As you are faithful to honor Him with thankful hearts, He will be faithful to honor you with even more blessings in return!

Here Is Your 3rd Harvest Key:
EVERYTHING BEGINS WITH A SEED!

Let me pray for you…

> *Heavenly Father, we believe that Your Word is true and that You will never fail to honor Your Covenants with us. Your plan was for all created things to begin with a Seed, and we agree with You that this was a good plan. Thank You for Your Word that is filled with Blessings for us as we continue to walk in a loving, faith-filled, obedient Covenant relationship with You. I pray that You would help Your child to understand and embrace the truth that everything begins with a Seed. Cause them to hear Your voice and respond to the leading of Your Holy Spirit regarding Sowing Uncommon Seeds and Reaping Your Uncommon Harvests. I pray this in Jesus' Name. Amen.*

Now be encouraged by this testimony of how God blessed Betty. And it all began with her Sowing an Uncommon $58 Seed!

'All My Pain Is Gone!'

"I knew nothing about the principles of Seedtime and Harvest until I watched one of your broadcasts, and God led me to Sow an Uncommon $58 Seed into your ministry. I have been

Sowing each month since then, and I'm being blessed in ways I never would have imagined!

"Shortly after I began Sowing my Seeds, I was miraculously healed of fibromyalgia, which I had suffered from terribly for 32 years. My fibromyalgia had been extremely painful and debilitating, but now all my pain is gone!

"Recently my daughter and I have developed a very close relationship, something I have prayed about for years. And I now have a new sense of the Holy Spirit guiding me and giving me peace like I've never experienced before. It's so wonderful to feel free and happy in the Lord!

"Thanks for being there for me and teaching me about God's Uncommon Harvests!" — **Betty**

My friend, what God has done for Betty, He can do for *you!*

I'm being blessed in ways I never would have imagined!

Small Seeds, Great Harvests

To what shall we liken the kingdom of God?
Or with what parable shall we picture it?
It is like a mustard seed which when it is sown
on the ground, is smaller than all the seeds on earth; but
when it is sown, it grows up and becomes greater than all
herbs, and shoots out large branches,
so that the birds of the air may nest under its shade.

—MARK 4:30–31

A shepherd brought his sling. A little boy brought his lunch. A widow brought her mite. They offered to God what they had, and it was enough…more than enough! Because of their faith and obedience, God honored their small Seeds and created great Harvests that brought huge blessings.

What Seeds are you holding in your hand today? Do they seem small and insignificant? Just as He did with a shepherd, a little boy, and a widow, when you release the Seed in your hand, God releases the Harvest in His hand.

A slingshot killed a giant. A lunch fed a multitude. And a small offering has reached across the centuries to impact millions in the Body of Christ. So, if what you're holding in your hand seems insignificant…if it's too small to be your Harvest…make it your Seed!

Make It Count

When we're afraid we don't have enough, we tend to hoard what we do have, fearing that if we let go of our little bit, we'll end up with nothing. But in God's economy, the very opposite is true: God will take the little we give Him, bless it, multiply it, and give it back to us as an Uncommon Harvest!

> *It's not the size of our gift that matters to Him: God is looking for our SACRIFICE.*

Zechariah 4:10 encourages us not to despise the day of *"small things."* Even if what we're giving to God seems small in our own eyes, we must be willing to Sow these humble gifts of our time, talent, or treasure back into His Kingdom. God knows how much or how little we have. Our willingness to trust and obey Him is what draws His attention.

It's not the size of our gift that matters to Him: God is looking for our SACRIFICE. Our Uncommon Seed gifts must cost us something. Scripture teaches us this truth in the example of King David in 2 Samuel 24.

David had angered the Lord by numbering the fighting soldiers he had available to him throughout Israel and Judah, revealing a pride in the extent of his kingship and a reliance on his army rather than a humble dependency on God. Convicted of his sin, David repented before the Lord, but he still suffered the consequences of his choices when God sent a plague that wiped out 70,000 of the 1,300,000 men David had been foolishly relying on.

To end the plague, the prophet Gad instructed David to build an altar to the Lord on the threshing floor of a Jebusite named Araunah. When Araunah saw the king approaching, he bowed before him and said, *"Why has my lord the king come to his servant?"*

David replied, *"To buy the threshing floor from you, to build an altar to the LORD, that the plague may be withdrawn from the people."*

Araunah responded, *"Let my lord the king take and offer up whatever seems good to him. Look, here are oxen for burnt sacrifice, and threshing implements and the yokes of the oxen for wood. All these, O king, Araunah has given to the king. May the LORD your God accept you."*

But rather than accepting Araunah's offer to give him everything he needed to build the altar and make the sacrifice, David said, *"No, but I will surely buy it from you for a price; nor will I offer burnt offerings to the LORD my God with that which costs me nothing."*

Scripture goes on to say, *"David bought the threshing floor and the oxen for fifty shekels of silver. And David built there an altar to the LORD, and offered burnt offerings and peace offerings. So the LORD heeded the prayers for the land, and the plague was withdrawn from Israel."*

David was the king, and he certainly could have demanded from Araunah anything he wanted. He could have built the altar and made the sacrifice to God for free. However, he knew his sacrifice had to cost him something. And because of his obedience and prayers, God stopped the plague.

In the same way, our sacrifices to God must cost us something. He notices. They matter to Him. Even the seemingly small or insignificant gifts are important to Him when they're important to us.

Big Doors Swing on Small Hinges

Perhaps you're thinking, "$58 worth of Seed isn't enough to Reap a Harvest from God!"

My friend, never underestimate God's power and desire to change our lives in an instant with something that may seem like it's too small to matter. The most powerful forces are often controlled by tiny objects we may never see.

Never underestimate God's power and desire to change our lives in an instant with something that may seem like it's too small to matter.

When people share their testimony with me about the major turning points of their lives, I'm often amazed to hear how a seemingly insignificant event can have such powerful impact. This was certainly true for me. Over 30 years ago, I was in a discount department store in Tulsa, Oklahoma, buying some things to decorate my dorm room at Oral Roberts University when I struck up a conversation with the attractive checkout girl. Not a big deal, right? We just had a little chat to pass the time while she rang up my order.

How was I to know that this lovely young woman was going to be my wife and the mother of our children? That supposedly "chance" meeting and our small conversation changed my life forever!

The Bible tells us that…

❦ A tiny rudder can turn a huge ship (James 3:4).

❦ The tongue is so small, yet it's like a little flame that can set a whole forest on fire (James 3:5).

❦ Mustard-seed faith can move a mountain (Matthew 17:20).

❦ The seemingly insignificant little town of Bethlehem became the birthplace of the Savior of the World (Matthew 2:4–6).

Does a $58 Uncommon Seed seem too small in your eyes? When God is involved, a little is all that is needed. He causes big doors to swing on small hinges! You can trust Him to do BIG things with a small Seed that's Sown in faith, obedience, and expectancy.

Jesus emphasizes this truth when He teaches His disciples the parable of the mustard seed:

> To what shall we liken the kingdom of God? Or with what parable shall we picture it? It is like a mustard seed which when it is sown on the ground, is smaller than all the seeds on earth; but when it is sown, it grows up and becomes greater than all herbs, and shoots out large branches, so that the birds of the air may nest under its shade (Mark 4:30–32).

The Lord knows we need encouragement. He knows how we tend to look at our need rather than at our Seed. This is why He reminds us that even the smallest seed in the world—the mustard seed—grows into a tree. Just imagine...if God can take a tiny mustard seed and produce a tree that becomes a massive birdhouse, what kind of a Harvest will He produce from your small Seed Sown in faith?

Seed Faith

When a farmer plants a tiny corn seed, he ends up with millions of corn kernels. In the same way, when you Sow small Seeds into God's Kingdom, He multiplies your Seed into a Harvest far greater than the original small Seed you Sowed. It's the same in the spiritual world as it is in the natural...

God will take the Uncommon Seeds you Sow and use them to create your Uncommon Harvests. Keep in mind that Seed faith is Sowing something God has given in order to receive something He's promised. A small Seed, Sown in faith, can produce a HUGE Harvest.

So what Seeds has God given YOU?

Right now, find a pen and with God's help, make a "Seed List" of the time, talent, and treasure He's given you. Don't worry about the size of the Seeds, just write them down.

Next, I want you to pray over this list. Ask the Lord to give you the desire, the opportunity, and the courage to faithfully Sow these Uncommon Seeds for an Uncommon Harvest.

Ask Him to take your small Seeds and multiply them into a great Harvest for His Kingdom and as a personal Harvest in your life:

Here Is Your 4ᵗʰ Harvest Key:

SMALL SEEDS CAN REAP GREAT HARVESTS!

Let me pray for you...

Heavenly Father, thank You that You love to bless us with Your Uncommon Harvests. We trust that what is meaningful to us is meaningful to You. Give Your child the confidence to Sow Uncommon Seeds into Your Kingdom that cost them something, regardless of their size. Please take and multiply their Seeds into great Harvests that further Your Kingdom and meet their every need. I pray this in Jesus' Name. Amen.

Now be encouraged by this testimony of how God blessed Betty, who Sowed small Uncommon Seeds into God's Kingdom and Reaped great Uncommon Harvests from Him!

'The Uncommon Harvests Keep Getting Better!'

"Earlier this year, I came across one of your broadcasts, and the speaker was inviting people to Sow an Uncommon $58 Seed into your ministry for 12 months. He said the Lord was going to bless those who committed to doing this. Although I was already tithing and giving offerings to my church, I felt like I was one of the people who needed to Sow that Seed, so I began giving my $58 check each month.

"I am a retired widow living on a fixed income. My son went through a divorce several years ago, and since then he has been living with me. He has also had some real financial struggles after losing his home and business, and he's now incurred a lot of debt. So when I called to Sow my Seed, I also requested prayer for him.

"A few months ago, I went on vacation, and when I returned, I called my bank to see what my account balance was. When I heard the amount, I couldn't believe it. Amazingly, I had *$17,000 more* than what I was supposed to have! Thinking that someone must have made a mistake, I went to the bank to tell them of their error.

He is full of surprises and wants to bless all of us exceedingly, abundantly, more than we could ever think or ask.

"Incredibly, I discovered that the extra money in my account was no mistake! Plus, shortly afterward, I learned that my monthly income would also be increasing by $360 a month.

"But the blessings didn't stop there! Astonishingly, a friend of my son has given him a job and is helping him pay off his debt.

"And the Uncommon Harvest keeps getting better. During the recent holiday season, some of my relatives who previously never wanted to get together for the holidays due to unresolved conflicts and tension agreed to get together this year. As a result, our family relationship is now being restored. God is so good! He is full of surprises and wants to bless all of us exceedingly, abundantly, more than we could ever think or ask.

"God is no respecter of persons. What He did for me, He is waiting to do for others. I challenge and encourage everyone to step out in faith by Sowing your Uncommon Seed to God, and see what Uncommon Harvest He will bring your way." — Betty

My friend, what God has done for Betty, He can do for *you!*

BLESSED

Give, and it will be given to you: good measure, pressed down, shaken together, and running over will be put into your bosom. For with the same measure that you use, it will be measured back to you.

LUKE 6:38

5 Let Go!

I once heard a story about two farmers facing hard times…

These two farmers—neighbors—looked out over their dry, dusty fields without much reason to hope. There'd been a drought the year before, and the money in the bank was nearly as dried up as the land in front of them.

But the coming year promised to be the worst yet. As another season of drought was predicted in the forecasts, both farmers turned their faces toward Heaven and asked God to send the rain.

Weeks passed. Still there was no rain. If asked, both of them would have said they had faith in God to answer their prayers. But only one of the farmers did something—

He climbed on his tractor…plowed his fields…and planted his seeds.

In time, God answered the farmers' prayers and sent the rain. But only one farmer reaped a harvest. Why? Because regardless of what he saw in the natural, he believed God would bless the seeds he planted in faith. He released the seeds from his hand, and God released the harvest in His hand.

In difficult economic times like these, it can be a real challenge to faithfully Sow our Uncommon Seeds into God's Kingdom. If we're afraid of not having enough, we can be tempted to hold on to whatever we have. And then when the devil comes stalking us like a roaring lion seeking to devour our health, finances, or relationships (1Peter 5:8), we cry out to God in desperation.

Because regardless of what he saw in the natural, he believed God would bless the seeds he planted in faith.

To overcome the devil's attacks, we must maintain an uninterrupted cycle of "letting go" of our Uncommon Seeds by Sowing bountifully into God's Kingdom. While the WORLD'S economic system tells us to hoard, GOD'S economy tells us to give. Instead of hoarding our Seed, He asks us to release back to Him what He has placed in our hands. Only then will we Reap His blessings in our lives and be covered by His supernatural provision and protection. What we Sow, He multiplies.

Think about it this way....

Let's say you put a handful of seed in a jar, stick the jar in a cupboard, and leave it there for three months. When you come back, what will you find? A jar of seed. You certainly wouldn't discover any kind of harvest growing in your kitchen cabinet! In order for those seeds to become a harvest, you would have to plant them in healthy soil.

The same is true in the spiritual realm. Unless you Sow your Seed, nothing happens. You must Sow them into Good Ground and then water them with your faith, obedience, and expectancy. Then you will Reap God's Uncommon Harvests!

LET GO | 53

It's Impossible to Out-Give God

God initiated this unending cycle of giving and receiving by giving us life. He gave us His only Son to be our Savior, and He gives us His Holy Spirit to be our Comforter and Guide. Everything we have is because of His compassion and generosity. God has established His eternal principle of Sowing and Reaping, and He never interrupts this cycle.

We do.

Everything we have, we only have because God has given it to us, and He wants us to express our gratitude and trust by giving back to Him a portion of what He has given us (Malachi 3:8–10). He gives us more, and we give back to Him again. Then He blesses us with even more. As He promises, God gives Seed to the SOWER (2 Corinthians 9:10).

Whenever we let go of what we're holding on to, He replaces it with something better. It's impossible to out-give God. His very nature is to give!

Some may argue, "Well, I've tried that, David, and it doesn't work. I've Sown and I haven't Reaped. I've given, and I've received nothing in return."

Beware of this faulty thinking. Satan is a liar, and he whispers lies of fear and doubt into our ears to cause us to hold on to our Seed instead of Sowing it back into God's Kingdom. The enemy doesn't want God's Kingdom to grow, and he doesn't want our lives to be blessed with God's Harvests!

Don't allow the devil to steal from you by tempting you to hold on to your Seeds of time, talent, and treasure. Unlike Satan,

God is NOT a liar. He speaks Truth, and His Word is Truth. Do you want to receive more of His blessings in your life? Give. Do you want to Reap His Harvests? Sow.

> *There is one who scatters, yet increases more;*
> *and there is one who withholds more than is right, but*
> *it leads to poverty. The generous soul will be made rich,*
> *and he who waters will also be watered himself*
> (Proverbs 11:24–25).

Holding on to your Seed only leads to poverty: However, God promises that Sowing your Seed leads to His blessings! Be careful to recognize His Harvest of Blessings when they come, because sometimes our Harvests will be in the form of money, and sometimes they will be blessings that money can't buy.

Bountiful Sowing = Bountiful Reaping!

When you first heard the Scriptural principle of Seedtime and Harvest, I believe something stirred in your heart as you sensed the Holy Spirit telling you that this is a "God Principle"— His truth for His people.

Sometimes our Harvests will be in the form of money, and sometimes they will be blessings that money can't buy.

My friend, don't allow the enemy to sow seeds of doubt in your mind. When you commit to Sowing Uncommon Seeds into God's Kingdom, you are being an obedient doer of the word and not a hearer only (James 1:22). You will become excited and full of hope as you expectantly wait to Reap God's Uncommon Harvest in your life. I urge you today to release the Uncommon Seed God has placed in your hands.

Here Is Your 5th Harvest Key:

WHEN YOU RELEASE THE SEED IN YOUR HAND, GOD RELEASES THE HARVEST IN HIS HAND!

Let me pray for you…

Heavenly Father, we want to be like the farmer who planted seeds, even in the midst of drought. Give us that kind of Seed faith. You ask us to trust You so that You can bless us. It's true that we can't out-give You. Father, help your child to Sow bountifully into Your Kingdom, so that they will Reap bountifully of Your Harvests. Give them the courage and the hope to release the Seed You've placed in their hand so that You can release the Harvests in Your hand. I pray this in Jesus' Name. Amen.

Now be encouraged by this testimony of how God blessed Karen, who released the Seed that was in her hand and Reaped the Harvest that was in His hand for her son!

'Greg Flat-Lined for 30 Minutes'

"Your ministry has stirred my faith, and I'm grateful for your prayers for me and my family. My son Greg, age 43, had a heart attack while staying on my couch one night. I tried to trust God during this ordeal, because I had been Sowing financial Seeds to Inspiration Ministries on his behalf, asking God to deliver him from alcoholism and congestive heart failure.

"I called the ambulance, and the EMTs rushed to Greg's side. However, he was unresponsive, and they decided there was no use to work on him any longer. By then he had already been unconscious for more than 30 minutes. At the very last moment, one of

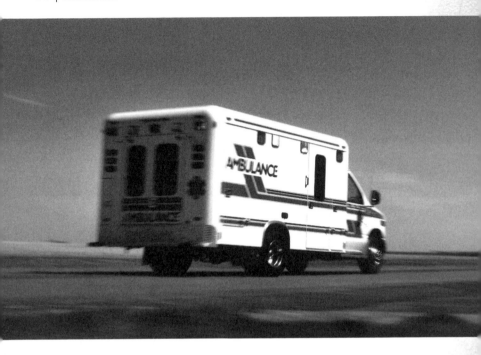

the EMTs said, 'I feel a faint pulse!' So they rushed Greg to the hospital, and I followed in my car. After he was examined by the emergency room doctor, I was told there was no way he could make it through the night.

"I stayed in the hospital emergency waiting room, awaiting further news. Finally, at 2:00 p.m. the following day, two doctors, a chaplain, a social worker, a nurse, and a nun all came into the family waiting room to tell us Greg had 'flat-lined' again for more than 30 minutes. They strongly recommended taking him off life support, saying he surely would have no brain function after being down more than 30 minutes twice.

"Upon convincing my ex-husband, our other son, and me that Greg couldn't possibly function after such events, we reluctantly went into his private room to say our good-byes. We all looked at Greg and wept. His face was swollen, purple, gray, and black. I said, 'I want to rub his feet before we go. He always loved that during his other hospital stays.'

"As I rubbed his feet and prayed, a strong sense of faith enveloped me. I stood up, cupped my hand on his cheek and said, 'Greg, it's Mom.' Immediately, he opened his eyes, sat up, and began to pull all the tubing from his body! We quickly called in the nurses to restrain him.

"All three nurses later told me they each had more than 20 years experience in the ICU, but they had never seen anything so astounding! The EMTs and emergency room doctor had to come in and see for themselves what had happened. They stood in disbelief as they looked at him. I believe this was a miracle, and I praise God daily for His goodness in sparing Greg's life!

As I prayed, a strong sense of faith enveloped me.

"Amazingly, Greg is being restored to full health. His doctors have taken him off the liver transplant list, and his heart and kidneys are now normal—though they had all shut down. Miraculously, his mind and memory are as sharp as ever.

"God bless your ministry. Your prayers and encouragement have been a great blessing to me." — **Karen**

My friend, what God has done for Karen, He can do for *you!*

BLESSED

*Other seeds fell
into the good soil,
and as they grew up
and increased,
they yielded a crop
and produced
thirty, sixty, and
a hundredfold.*

MARK 4:8 (NASB)

6 Good Ground

If you've ever taken a car ride through the countryside, you've probably passed acre after acre of abundant, thriving farm-land. You can almost imagine those healthy green crops just springing up out of the rich, dark earth.

But bountiful harvests like that don't just happen, do they?

Behind every ripe harvest field stands a wise farmer who has carefully cultivated and prepared that ground before he ever planted a single seed.

He spent time removing the rocks, putting proper nutrients into the soil, and making sure there would be proper irrigation and drainage. He did everything he knew to do to maximize the har-vest he expected his land to yield. Seed is costly…and that's why the farmer did all he could to ensure a good harvest before sowing his precious seed.

How does the farmer know whether or not he made a wise decision about his soil? By the harvest he reaps in the fall!

Jesus perfectly illustrates the value of Sowing Seed into Good Ground in the parable He told about the sower who went out to sow (Matthew 13:3–23). Some of the seeds fell by the wayside, and birds came and ate it. Other seeds fell on stony ground and eventually withered away because they couldn't put down strong healthy roots, while still other seeds fell on thorny ground and got choked out. But some of the seeds fell on *"good ground and yielded a crop; some a hundred-fold, some sixty, some thirty."*

How does the farmer know whether or not he made a wise decision about his soil? By the harvest he reaps in the fall!

After telling the story, Jesus gave His disciples this explanation: *"But he who received seed on the good ground is he who hears the word and understands it, who indeed bears fruit and produces: some a hundredfold, some sixty, some thirty"* (v. 23).

Is All Ground GOOD Ground?

Keep in mind that not all soil yields the same level of Harvest. Just because it may look good at first glance, closer examination may reveal that the spiritual ground is dry, infested, rocky, hard, or unproductive. The quality of the spiritual soil is definitely going to affect the quantity and quality of the Harvest.

YOUR SEED + POOR SOIL = A POOR HARVEST!

YOUR SEED + GOOD GROUND = A GREAT HARVEST!

Why would you want to waste your prayers and financial Seeds by Sowing them into soil that isn't going to yield a fruitful Harvest in your personal life, and even more importantly, yield little or nothing for God's eternal Kingdom? Seeds are too precious to waste! If you're like me, you want the Seeds you Sow of your time, talent, and treasure to Reap a 100-fold return. We receive this by Sowing our Seed into Ground where we'll Reap the greatest rewards.

Wise and faithful Sowing into Good Ground will always prosper you, so it's important to Sow your UNCOMMON Seed into Good Ground that will produce the greatest amount of fruit!

So When Is Ground Good?

Interestingly, we also learn from this parable that not even all Good Ground is the same. Some produces a 30-fold return, some 60, and some a 100-fold return.

When God truly anoints a ministry, it becomes Good Ground for Sowing. With Good Ground, you are assured of Reaping a great Harvest. Ask yourself these "fruit" questions about any church or ministry into which you are considering Sowing your precious Seeds:

❧ Is the Word of God preached without compromise?
❧ Is Jesus Christ exalted as Lord and Savior?
❧ Is honor given to the Holy Spirit and His gifts and fruit?
❧ Are the Lost saved and Believers discipled?
❧ Are lives eternally impacted for God's Kingdom?
❧ Is genuine love expressed for the Lord and others?

If your answer to even one of these questions is, "No," then you probably don't want to waste your precious Seeds by Sowing them into what could very well be rocky, hard, or unproductive soil.

However, if you can answer, "Yes!" to all of these questions, then you most likely have found fruitful Ground into which you can faithfully Sow your precious Seed, trusting God to release the Harvests He has destined for your life.

Remember that TIME is a key ingredient between Sowing and Reaping. You can't plant a garden today and make a salad tomorrow! In the same way that seeds in the natural take time to produce a harvest, the Uncommon Seeds you Sow into God's Kingdom usually take time to produce His Uncommon Harvests in your life.

Patiently wait and you will joyfully Reap!

Patiently wait and you will joyfully Reap! Meditate on this verse and then stand by faith on God's Word: *"Those who sow in tears shall reap in joy. He who continually goes forth weeping, bearing seed for sowing, shall doubtless come again with rejoicing, bringing his sheaves with him"* (Psalm 126:5–6).

Sacred Seeds

In the Old Testament, when the Temple priests presented the Israelites' offerings to God, they first would ceremonially prepare themselves. He commanded them to wash, remove their shoes, and wear spotless garments. There was a sense of holiness and sacredness as they solemnly offered to Him what He required.

In the same way, as we obediently bring God our offerings, we, too, must prepare ourselves. King David addressed this in Psalm 24:3–4 when he wrote, *"Who may ascend into the hill of the LORD? Or who may stand in His holy place? He who has clean hands and a pure heart, who has not lifted up his soul to an idol, nor sworn deceitfully."*

As we are faithful to Sow our Seeds into God's Kingdom with *"clean hands and a pure heart,"* God will honor our offerings and we *"shall receive blessing from the LORD, and righteousness from the God of his salvation"* (v. 5).

Sadly, in our church services today, we too often tend to rush through the passing of the collection plate as though this part of our worship were something to do quickly and get it over with so we can move on to the message or the next praise song. Our motivation for giving must be out of love for the Lord, love for His Word, love for His Kingdom, and love for the Lost who will be reached through our sacrificial giving. The presentation of our financial Seeds needs to be a solemn and joyful act of worship to the Lord!

As you Sow your Uncommon Seeds and water them with your love, faith, and obedience, "doubtless" you WILL rejoice and Reap God's Uncommon Harvests!

Whose Table Are You Eating From?

When prayerfully deciding where to Sow your Seeds, consider where you are being fed.

Malachi 3:10 tells us to bring our tithes into *"the storehouse."* Many Christians erroneously have been taught that the storehouse is simply the local church. This is an inaccurate description and definition of what the storehouse represents in Scripture.

Give where you are being spiritually fed!

In the Bible, the storehouse signified a place where things were kept for the service, offerings, and sacrifices of the Temple. When something was needed for the Temple, the priests would go into the storehouse to retrieve some of the resources that had been deposited there.

The message for us is clear: You have a spiritual account in Heaven, and every time you Sow your financial Seeds into the Good

Ground of God's Kingdom, you are storing up treasures in that account. When you need something in your life, there should be "storehouses" where you've made deposits that you can draw upon.

When you eat lunch at McDonald's, you don't go across the street to Wendy's to pay for your meal! Yet this is exactly what many Christians do when they Sow their financial Seeds into churches or ministries that aren't feeding them spiritually.

I'll never forget one man's response when I asked why he had planted a large Seed into Inspiration Ministries. He told me, "David, it's because I eat at your table every day!" So the answer to the question of "Where should I give my tithes and offerings?" is this: Give where you are being spiritually fed!

If you're being fed by your local church and by one or more different ministries, then divide your Seeds—your tithes and your offerings—among them. I encourage you to Sow your Seed into ministries that truly are nourishing your spirit.

Here Is Your 6th Harvest Key:
SOW YOUR SEED INTO GOOD GROUND!

Let me pray for you…

Heavenly Father, thank You for Your Word that is full of wisdom for us regarding Sowing and Reaping. Make us wise stewards of the Seeds You have entrusted to us. Please give Your child the ability to discern the "Good Ground" that You have prepared to receive their precious Seed. As they Sow their Seed into Your Kingdom, I ask that You would cause it to Reap a 100-fold return, both in their personal life and in Your eternal Kingdom, that

they may be blessed and be a blessing, and that You would
be glorified. I pray this in Jesus' Name. Amen.

Now be encouraged by this testimony of how God blessed Sharon, who Sowed her Uncommon Seeds into God's Kingdom through the Good Ground of Inspiration Ministries and Reaped an Uncommon 100-fold Harvest from Him!

'The Money Kept Pouring In!'

"I'm a divorced mother with three children, and I Sowed my first Seed into your ministry when things were very hard for us.

"The bill collectors were coming to our door, and the situation appeared hopeless. But I reminded the Lord that I had Sown into the Good Ground of your ministry and that I'm a giver, like He is.

I praise God
for my Harvest of
financial miracles,
and I'm excited about
being a lifetime
Inspiration Partner.

"The next day I was feeling discouraged as I went to an ATM machine to withdraw a small amount of money. I was shocked to see that my account suddenly held 2000 British pounds!

"Then the money kept pouring in. The government sent me 3000 more pounds as an unexpected tax refund. Next, my ex-husband came into a financial windfall and finally was able to catch up on a large amount of money he owed me!

"I praise God for my Harvest of financial miracles, and I'm excited about being a lifetime Inspiration Partner." — **Sharon**

My friend, what God has done for Sharon, He can do for *you!*

7 Be Specific!

The bowl of flour was not used up,
nor did the jar of oil run dry, according to the word
of the LORD which He spoke by Elijah.
—1 KINGS 17:16

In the natural world, God has authorized seeds to mature into a harvest by assigning each one a specific set of invisible genetic instructions called DNA to determine what it will be when it matures. He has assigned...

❧ An acorn to become an oak tree
❧ An apple seed to become an apple tree
❧ A father's seed to become a child

In the same way, you must give your Uncommon Seeds authority to multiply and grow into an Uncommon Harvest by giving them a spiritual DNA—a **Specific Assignment**—for the Uncommon Harvest you want to Reap. There's a powerful story in 1 Kings 17 that illustrates this simple principle.

God had led His prophet, Elijah, into the wilderness to live by the Brook Cherith. There the Lord had provided him with rest, food, and water. But eventually the water in that stream had slowly dried because there was a severe drought in the land. So the Lord sent Elijah to Zarephath and told him a widow living there would provide for him.

Elijah obeyed God, and by the time he got to Zarephath, he was thirsty and hungry. When he encountered the widow, she was gathering sticks to make a cooking fire, and he asked her for a drink of water and something to eat.

However, due to the drought, there was a great famine, and the widow's situation was desperate. All of her resources—her husband, her money, even her hope for any kind of future—were gone. According to verse 12, she had just enough flour in her bowl and oil in her jar to make a morsel of bread for herself and her son, and then she assumed both of them were going to starve to death.

You must give your Uncommon Seeds authority to multiply and grow into an Uncommon Harvest by giving them a spiritual DNA—a Specific Assignment.

Elijah's response to her terrible situation is pretty startling. Rather than feeling sorry for her or trying to find something for her to eat, he told her to make him some bread first, and then make something for her and her son out of whatever was left. Elijah promised the woman if she would listen to what he told her to do, her bowl of flour and her jar of oil would not run out.

The prophet's request to provide for him before meeting her and her son's needs must have seemed very greedy and selfish to this desperate mother. What he was telling her to do would have seemed beyond difficult. Impossible. Foolish!

But God had a different perspective. He wasn't planning this woman's demise. He had an Uncommon Harvest of Blessings on His mind for her, and so He had sent His prophet to her with a life-giving instruction, one that she could obey or ignore.

Making the Right Choice

At that moment, this single mom had a choice to make. She could believe what the man of God was telling her to do, or she could have one last meal with her boy, and then lie down and wait for them both to die. She could have said, "No!" She could have said, "Leave me alone!" She could have said, "Go get your own bread!"

But she didn't.

She chose to believe Elijah, obey his instruction, and then wait with hope-filled expectation for what the man of God had promised to come true. The result of her wise choice is in verses 15 and 16:

This single mom had a choice to make. She could believe what the man of God was telling her to do, or she could have one last meal with her boy, and then lie down and wait for them both to die.

> *So she went and did according to the word of Elijah, and she and he and her household ate for many days. The bowl of flour was not exhausted nor did the jar of oil become empty, according to the word of the LORD which He spoke through Elijah.*

Because Elijah knew the widow's handful of flour and few drops of oil weren't enough to be a life-giving Harvest, he had given authority to the spiritual DNA of those flour and oil "Seeds" by giving them a **Specific Assignment**: for God to take them and turn them into a Harvest of provision for this little family.

And because this woman made the right choice and Sowed an Uncommon Seed in the face of desperate need, she went from having "not enough" to having "more than enough." From facing death to enjoying an abundant life.

The widow chose to trust and release what was in her hand. The result? Miraculous provision as God released His Harvest of Blessings into her desperate circumstances. Had she hoarded the little bit in her hands, the consequences would have been terrible. But this mother and son ate, and ate well, and ate every day, for many days. Throughout the remaining years of drought and famine, her flour was never used up, and her oil never ran dry.

Your Future Is in Your Hands!

My friend, you also can make the right choice and experience this same kind of blessing. Whatever your need may be—financial provision, healing, restoration of a relationship—the One who loves you can meet your need.

> *Your future will be decided by whom and by what you choose to believe, and your choices will determine what you will Reap.*

Just as He did for the widow, God also has an unlimited supply for YOU. In the midst of the difficult circumstances you're facing, you can obey His Word and believe all of His promises are for you. Your future will be decided by whom and by what you choose to believe, and your choices will determine what you will Reap. Your faith-filled obedience can be the difference between poverty and prosperity, between death and life.

As long as you hold onto your Seed, you will never experience a Harvest greater than what you're holding. But as you release the Seed in your hand, God will release the Harvest in His hand. When you put God first...when you look to Him as your Source and give out of your need as the widow did, then get ready for God to move supernaturally in your situation.

Is there a specific Uncommon Harvest you need to Reap? Then like Elijah, when you Sow your Uncommon Seeds, be sure to give them authority by giving each one a **Specific Assignment**. The same God who supernaturally multiplied the flour and oil for the widow will supply what you need and multiply what you Sow!

Your Seed's Specific Assignment can be for healing, the restoration of a relationship, wisdom, a financial need, employment...whatever area of your life in which you need God to move on your behalf. Consistently water your Seed with faith, obedience, and expectation for God to do what He says in His Word He'll do. Then watch Him step into your circumstances as He releases His Uncommon Harvests in your life!

Here Is Your 7*th* Harvest Key:

GIVE YOUR SEED AUTHORITY...GIVE IT A SPECIFIC ASSIGNMENT!

Let me pray for you...

Heavenly Father, thank You for using the natural world to teach us powerful spiritual lessons. We believe in Your goodness, love, and faithfulness as we Sow our Uncommon Seeds into Your Kingdom. I pray the Prayer of Agreement from Matthew 18:19 over Your child, that as they give their Seeds authority by giving them a Specific Assignment, they will Reap Your specific Uncommon Harvests in their circumstances. We're grateful for Your

*love and mercy, and we choose to trust You and the prom-
ises of Your Word. I pray this in Jesus' name. Amen.*

Now be encouraged by this testimony of how God blessed
Gloria, who gave her Uncommon Seed a Specific Assignment and
then Reaped a Specific Uncommon Harvest from Him!

'God Restored Our Family!'

"My husband and I had been praying for our daughter for a
long time. She had turned away from the Lord, and her life was in
shambles. Eventually her marriage ended, she lost her job, and her

*I requested prayer
for my daughter
and gave my Seed
the Assignment to
bring her back
to God.*

life spun out of control even more. But we refused to give up on her and kept praying she would turn back to Christ.

"One day while watching your 'Uncommon Harvest' special, we heard about the power of Sowing an Uncommon Seed into God's Kingdom, giving it a Specific Assignment, then trusting God to do a miracle. Stepping out in faith, I called Inspiration Ministries and began Sowing my financial Seed. I requested prayer for my daughter, and gave my Seed the assignment to bring her back to God.

"Soon miracles began taking place! First, my daughter gave her life back to Jesus. Then God opened a door for her to get a new job. Praise God, He has restored our family!"
— Gloria

My friend, what God has done for Gloria, He can do for *you!*

BLESSED

Do not withhold
good from those
to whom it is due,
when it is in your
power to do it.

PROVERBS 3:27 (NASB)

8 Make It Happen

D o you remember the "Golden Rule" you were taught as a child?

When we were mean to other kids, our parents would sternly reprimand us, **"Do unto others as you would have them do unto you!"** They were teaching us that we needed to treat others the same way we wanted to be treated. We were to share our toys with others, because we wanted them to share their toys with us. We weren't to kick or punch others, because we didn't want them to kick or punch us.

Jesus Himself taught us this important principle in Matthew 7:12, and it applies whether you're a kid on the playground or an adult on the job.

But did you know that in His Word, God has another "Golden Rule"…one that specifically applies to Sowing Uncommon Seeds and Reaping God's Uncommon Harvests?

*"With goodwill doing service as to the Lord, and not to men, knowing that **whatever good anyone does, he will receive the same from the Lord**"* (Ephesians 6:7–8).

In other words: What you make happen for others, God makes happen for you! The Bible is full of stories demonstrating this principle:

- ❧ God blessed Abraham and Sarah with a child of their own *after* they prayed for God to remove barrenness from the king's household (Genesis 20).
- ❧ God honored King David's life *after* he honored the life of King Saul (1 Samuel 26).
- ❧ God gave Nehemiah authority and resources for rebuilding Jerusalem's walls *after* he faithfully served in the house of a pagan king (Nehemiah 2).

We're to serve the Lord by doing good things for others, and when we do, the Lord will do good things for us. When we Sow Uncommon Seeds of our time, talent, and treasure into people's lives, we Reap His Uncommon Harvests. As we bless others—our family, friends, pastor, church, coworkers, boss, and yes, even our enemies—He blesses us abundantly in return.

What you make happen for others, God makes happen for you!

From His vast wealth throughout the whole universe, God pours out His blessings on His children who are walking in a loving, obedient, faith-filled Covenant Relationship with Him—a Covenant Relationship that includes God's eternal principle of Sowing and Reaping. As we Sow into the lives of others, we Reap God's Harvests in our own lives.

What Ruth *Did for* Naomi, God *Did for* Ruth!

This truth is evident in the story of a simple country girl from the plains of Moab.

We learn in the book of Ruth that Naomi and her husband Elimelech, along with their two sons Mahlon and Chilion, lived in Bethlehem, Judah. However, when a terrible famine struck the land, the family moved to the neighboring country of Moab. But the hard times didn't end there…in fact, things grew worse. First Elimelech died. Then after their marriages to two Moabite women—Ruth and Orpah—Naomi's two sons died as well.

Naomi wanted no more of the suffering she had encountered in Moab, and since the famine had ended in her own country, she decided to return home. Instructing her daughters-in-law to return to their own families, Naomi intended to travel to Bethlehem alone. But while Orpah reluctantly went back to her own people, Ruth refused to leave her mother-in-law.

Even though her own husband had also died, Ruth rejected the easy road leading back to her childhood home. Instead, she chose to follow her mother-in-law, Naomi, to an unfamiliar place. Even though Naomi was bitter and going through a dark time in her life, Ruth refused to leave her, no matter how tough things got.

Ruth repeatedly demonstrated her dedication and devotion to Naomi. She worked hard in the fields to bring home food and showed tremendous respect for her mother-in-law. Her unswerving faithfulness in standing by Naomi led the women of the Bethlehem community to say to her that Ruth was *"better to (her) than seven sons"* (4:15).

Ruth endured much adversity to bless Naomi, and in the midst of her suffering, **God blessed Ruth.**

Naomi had a relative, Boaz, who was *"a man of standing"* (Ruth 2:1). Not only did he help Ruth as she gathered grain in his fields, he also chose to "redeem" the family land from Naomi and marry Ruth. God gave Ruth and Boaz a son, and through him, the lineage of King David was established...and the Savior of the world, Jesus Christ, was born.

Ruth prospered in her own day, and she continues to be honored for her faithfulness and remembered thousands of years beyond her lifetime—an Uncommon Harvest indeed!

When *YOU* Bless Others, God Blesses *YOU!*

Do you want God to bless you with His Uncommon Harvests? Then be a blessing to others by Sowing your Uncommon Seed! Seek God's Kingdom first, and then all the blessings He has planned for your life will be added to you (Matthew 6:33).

Consider this...

Are you a Problem Creator or a Problem Solver? A person who creates problems...

- ❧ Makes life harder for those around them
- ❧ Creates mountains out of molehills
- ❧ Criticizes, judges, and discourages others
- ❧ Demands that others bless them!

However, a person who solves problems...

- ❧ Makes life easier for those around them
- ❧ Creates molehills out of mountains
- ❧ Affirms, accepts, and encourages others
- ❧ Blesses *others!*

In every circumstance, you can choose to make a situation better or worse. You can be an encourager or a discourager. You can offer compassionate assistance, or you can withhold your help. Do you want God to bless you? Then be a blessing!

Keep in mind that your Seed is anything that blesses others, while your Harvest is anything that blesses you. Concentrate on Sowing Seeds of your time, talent, and treasure to create successful situations for others. Be "other-centered" rather than "self-centered." Get involved with someone else's dream, and God will get involved with your dream!

Seek God's Kingdom first, and then all the blessings He has planned for your life will be added to you (Matthew 6:33).

Also, don't expect your Uncommon Harvest to come from where you have Sown: Look to God for your Uncommon Harvest because you have Sown! Your Harvest of Blessings most likely won't come from those you have blessed. He will ask you to Sow into another's field, and when it's His time for you to receive your Harvest, you'll most likely Reap from a different field.

Remember this: ALL Harvests belong to God, *"for ALL that is in heaven and in earth is Yours"* (1 Chronicles 29:11). He alone determines when—and where—we will Reap.

Here Is Your 8th Harvest Key:

WHAT YOU MAKE HAPPEN FOR OTHERS, GOD MAKES HAPPEN FOR YOU!

Let me pray for you…

Heavenly Father, thank You that You have created us in Your image, and that You have made us to be like You.

I ask You to please help Your child continue to grow in Your likeness; that just as You love to bless us, their desire to be a blessing to others would continually grow. May the Uncommon Seeds of time, treasure, and talent they Sow into Your Kingdom Reap a great Harvest of blessing in the lives of others, even as You pour out Your blessings on this precious one. I pray this in Jesus' Name. Amen.

Now be encouraged by this testimony of how God blessed Patti, who Sowed Uncommon Seeds to bless others and received God's blessing in her own life!

'The Uncommon Harvests Keep Getting Better!'

I'm so grateful for Inspiration Ministries, which is my oasis in the desert.

A Breakthrough in the Desert!

"I can't thank you enough for Inspiration Ministries! I live in Tucson, Arizona, which I often refer to as the 'backside of the desert.' And until I discovered INSP, my life was dry and empty, just like the desert.

"After giving birth to my daughter, I suffered a long and severe bout with postpartum depression and anxiety attacks. I didn't see this attack coming, and it was extremely debilitating. My baby daughter cried day and night because of stomach problems, and I was so depressed I wanted to die.

"Realizing that only God could free me from this paralyzing bondage, I rededicated my life to Christ. That's when the Lord led me to INSP. My faith grew and grew as I watched your programs and saw testimonies of people who had received miracles from God. Then one day I realized that I could have wonderful miracles happen in my life too!

"So I kept watching your programs and started seeking God for the things I wanted Him to do in my life. First the postpartum depression began to go away, and then I was recruited to lead praise and worship for the kids at my church.

"Soon I began choreographing dances to the children's worship songs. This was a miracle, because I have no training or experience in this. Yet the Lord guided and blessed me so much that I was hired as the Children's Programs Worship Director! It was like God gave me an 'Extreme Life Makeover'—spiritually and in every other way!

"After I started working again, God led me to Sow financial Seeds into your ministry, for I've been so richly blessed and nourished through your broadcasts. I always laugh when I hear you say you want to reach people in the 'remote places of the earth,' because that was me—suffering postpartum depression here on the backside of the desert!

> *"Now, thanks to God, my life is no longer dry and depressing. I'm so grateful for Inspiration Ministries, which is my oasis in the desert—a spiritual haven whenever I need encouragement and strength. Thank you!"* — **Patti**

My friend, what God has done for Patti, He can do for *you!*

This Means War!

He who is in you is greater than he who is in the world.

—1 JOHN 4:4

The devil hates God's principle of Seedtime and Harvest!

In Genesis 3, God walked with Adam and Eve in the garden. He fulfilled every need and gave them dominion over all that He had made...including the enemy. But the Word says that *"the serpent was more crafty than any beast of the field"* (Genesis 3:1). He was jealous of the favor God showed to the man and woman, and so he set out to deceive and control them. And rather than saying, *"Get behind me, Satan!"* (Matthew 16:23), Adam and Eve took the enemy's bait—hook, line, and sinker.

They ate from the forbidden tree and tried to hide from God. As a result, they suffered the natural consequences of their turning away from Him—a loss of abundance and the intimacy they had freely experienced with the Lord.

From the very beginning of creation, we see how the devil has tried to disguise himself as "harmless." Throughout history, we

have failed to discern the enemy's lies and manipulation and neg-
lected to exercise our God-given authority over him.

The truth is the devil is real and his power is real. He wants
nothing more than to see us miserable and separated from our
Savior. He is a liar and is the father of all lies (John 8:44). His goal
is to divide us from the truth of the Word and conquer us with his
deception. He comes to *"steal, kill, and destroy"* (John 10:10)…to
take away God's Harvest of Blessings and leave us with nothing.
His goal is ALWAYS to devour God's Seed:

- Moses was God's Seed, the deliverer God raised up to
  lead the Israelites to freedom in the Promised Land. So
  when Moses was born, Satan tried to devour God's Seed
  by killing all of the Jewish male babies (Exodus 1:15–17).
- Jesus is God's Seed, the Deliverer God has raised up to
  lead all Believers to Eternal freedom in our Promised
  Land. So when Jesus was born, Satan tried to devour
  God's Seed by once again murdering thousands of Jewish
  male babies (Matthew 2:16-18).
- And Satan is still trying to devour *your* God-given Seed
  and rob you of God's Harvest Blessings of power, peace,
  and provision.

However, the good news is that Satan WAS the ruler of this
world. He HAD dominion over the earth. However, through Jesus'
sinless life, sacrificial death on the Cross, and resurrection from the
dead, He stripped Satan of his authority and returned to us what
was lost when Adam and Even sinned in the Garden.

When Jesus Christ is our Lord and Savior and we're walking
in an obedient Covenant Relationship with God, we have the right
to take authority over the enemy. The challenge is that too often,

we don't act like we have the right to rule over Satan and instead allow him to rule over us.

But you only allow someone to rule over you if you think they have authority over you. Satan has deceived Believers into thinking he has the power, but he does not. Jesus has given us the keys to God's Kingdom (Matthew 16:19). We have the power!

You're Fighting in Two Worlds!

For your Seed to become your Harvest, you MUST wage war with the enemy. But sadly, too many Believers today are passive when it comes to spiritual warfare, and the devil is having a heyday in the Body of Christ with our health, finances, and relationships.

> *For your Seed to become your Harvest, you MUST wage war with the enemy.*

Most of us don't realize we're living in two different worlds: the NATURAL WORLD, where we use our five senses to see, touch, taste, hear, and smell…and the SPIRITUAL WORLD, where a fierce battle continually rages for the souls of mankind *"in the heavenly places"* (Ephesians 6:12).

It's in the SPIRITUAL WORLD where Satan works to control us by influencing what we think and the standards we live by. That's one reason it's so important to be careful about what we put into our minds…what we *"dwell on"* (Philippians 4:8–9).

And the truth is that the SPIRITUAL WORLD is more real than the NATURAL WORLD! Our world is dying, and everything in it will one day be GONE!

> *For all that is in the world—the lust of the flesh, the lust of the eyes, and the pride of life—is not of the Father*

*but is of the world. And the world is passing away, and the
lust of it; but he who does the will of God abides forever*
(1 John 2:16–17).

But in the meantime, we can't remain on the defensive when
it comes to spiritual warfare and just sit and wait for the enemy to
attack. Jesus tells us in Luke 10:19, *"Behold, I have given you
authority to tread on serpents and scorpions, and over all the power of
the enemy."* We must take the battle to devil—without fear! Be
encouraged and empowered by these words:

> *No weapon formed against you shall prosper, and every
> tongue which rises against you in judgment you shall con-
> demn. This is the heritage of the servants of the* LORD, *and
> their righteousness is from me,' says the* LORD (1 John 4:4).

What a powerful truth! Satan's weapons and accusations are
nothing when Jesus Christ lives within you. You have His strength,
His power, and His righteousness to use against the devil!

It's Time to Get Serious!

Jesus warns that the Kingdom of Heaven suffers violence,
and violent people take it by force (Matthew 11:12). We must start
using the spiritual weapons of warfare He's given us: faith, prayer,
worship, and the Word. Instead of having a defensive strategy
against the enemy, we must have an offensive battle plan to protect
what is rightfully ours as God's children and to take back what the
devil has stolen from us!

God has delegated His authority to His Son, who in turn has
delegated His authority to us: *"All authority has been given to Me in
heaven and earth...Peace to you. As the Father has sent Me, I also send*

you" (Matthew 28:18; John 20:21). Jesus is saying, "Just like My Dad sent Me, now I'm sending you with My power and authority." He's sending us out as the enemy's adversary.

An adversary is someone who actively, aggressively, and offensively opposes an enemy. When we're walking in a Covenant Relationship with God, He works through us to conquer evil. It's time for the Body of Christ—for you and me— to get serious and together actively, aggressively, and offensively oppose the devil!

> Walk in Jesus' authority, by living in a loving, faith-filled, obedient Covenant Relationship with God.

Jesus also said what we bind on this earth will be bound in Heaven, and what we loose on this earth will be loosed in Heaven (Matthew 16:19). However, this won't happen unless we exercise the authority we've been given.

But be careful…the devil isn't as concerned with the words we're shooting at him as he is concerned with WHO is shooting the words. If we're not right with God…if we have secret sin in our lives…if we're not obeying His Word and the voice of His Holy Spirit…then we can't expect the enemy to pay a whole lot of attention to who we are or what we say.

You have a choice today: You can sit back, do nothing, and let the enemy devour your Uncommon Seed and steal, kill, and destroy your Uncommon Harvest. Or, you can take up your weapons of spiritual warfare and begin to wage war against the enemy in the name of the Lord Jesus Christ!

Walk in Jesus' authority, by living in a loving, faith-filled, obedient Covenant Relationship with God. Obedience isn't always easy. But Scripture assures us, *"Therefore submit to God. Resist the devil and he will flee from you"* (James 4:7). Remember: God hasn't given you a spirit of fear, but He has given you a spirit of love, power, and a sound mind (2 Timothy 1:7)!

Here Is Your 9th Harvest Key:

FOR YOUR SEED TO BECOME A HARVEST, YOU MUST WAGE WAR WITH THE ENEMY!

Let me pray for you…

> *Heavenly Father, thank You that You have not left us alone and defenseless against the onslaught of the devil's attacks. You have given us spiritual weapons of warfare for us to fight against his onslaught. According to Psalm 18, You arm us with strength, teach us to make war, and deliver us from the enemy. I ask You now to cause a boldness to rise up within Your child to wage war with Your enemy. Protect their precious Seed so that Satan cannot devour it. Cause their Seeds Sown into Your Kingdom to flourish and grow into an Uncommon Harvest in their life and for Your eternal Kingdom. Thank You for the Blood of Your Son which covers, empowers, and protects. I pray this in Jesus' Name. Amen.*

Now be encouraged by this testimony of how God blessed Ramon and his wife as they waged war with the enemy by Sowing Uncommon Seeds into the Kingdom for their prodigal son and Reaped God's Uncommon Harvests!

'We're Celebrating a Great Victory in Our Son's Life!'

"Our son was a college student, and the devil was pulling him away from God. He had been a devout Christian as a child, even bringing others to Christ before Satan took him captive during his teenage years. My husband and I suffered deeply as he drifted further and further from the Lord.

"During the eight tearful years of our son's deception, we discovered Inspiration Ministries and began watching your programs. We began to understand the Word of God more deeply and started ed honoring the Lord by Sowing Uncommon Seeds for Souls. We prayerfully gave our financial Seeds a Specific Assignment for our son to return to Jesus.

Nothing in the world could ever replace the joy of seeing our son follow the Lord!

"Today, we're thrilled to report that our son has come back to the Lord! He asked forgiveness for all the pain he caused us, and he got rid of everything associated with his prodigal ways. Upon graduation from college, he even decided to spend several days alone to seek God and read His Word before jumping right into a career.

We're so grateful God answered our prayers...

"We're so grateful God answered our prayers and returned our son to us and to His ways. Nothing in the world could ever replace the joy of seeing our son follow the Lord!

> *"We know we wouldn't be celebrating this great victory in our son's life if it had not been for your faithful prayers and remarkable teachings about God's principle of Seedtime and Harvest. Thank you for all you are doing to change the lives of people everywhere!"* — **Ramon**

My friend, what God has done for Ramon and his family, He can do for *you!*

10 Wait Patiently... It's Coming!

I wait for the LORD, my soul waits,
and in His word I do hope.

—PSALM 130:5

Even when we've believed God, obeyed Him, and waited expectantly for Him to release His breakthroughs over our circumstances, God's Harvests may seem to be delayed. Often, we haven't Reaped His Harvests because it isn't His timing to release them yet.

But sometimes, God hasn't released His blessings because He's waiting for us to obey Him in one or more areas of our lives. Let me share some thoughts with you to encourage you to faithfully and obediently Sow your Seeds, so that you can joyfully Reap His Harvests:

- ❦ When you ask God for a HARVEST, He'll ask you for a SEED.
- ❦ Your Seed is WHAT God multiplies. Your obedience is WHY He multiplies it.
- ❦ If you obey Him in the DIFFICULT, God will do the IMPOSSIBLE.

Look to God and His Word for the courage you need to believe Him, obey Him, and wait expectantly for Him to move on your behalf. When you do, this is His promise to you:

> *For he who sows to his flesh will of the flesh reap corruption, but he who sows to the Spirit will of the Spirit reap everlasting life. And let us not grow weary while doing good, for in due season we shall reap if we do not lose heart* (Galatians 6:8–9).

Seasons of Change

Ecclesiastes 3:1 says, *"To every thing there is a season, a time for every purpose under heaven."* Nothing stays the same. Change is inevitable. The farmer knows there are definite seasons of seedtime and harvest...

❧ Spring is when he sows his seeds.
❧ Summer is when he waits for his crops to grow.
❧ Autumn is when he reaps what he has sown.
❧ Winter is when it can be cold, dark, and dreary, and nothing seems to be happening; it's during this season that the farmer waits and prepares for the coming spring.

Each of these seasons is vital; none is more important than another. It's the same in the spiritual world. The Uncommon Seeds you've Sown into God's Kingdom take time to sprout and grow into an Uncommon Harvest.

You must remember God Himself established the eternal principle of Seedtime and Harvest: *"While the earth remains, seedtime and harvest...shall not cease"* (Genesis 8:22). Be encouraged! The

Bible is clear: You WILL Reap what you Sow. Harvest time WILL come: *"He that goes forth and weeping, bearing precious seed, shall doubtless come again with rejoicing, bringing his sheaves [harvest] with him"* (Psalm 126:6).

Let Your Roots Grow Deep

Depending on where we live in the world, the winter season often brings with it a cold and dreary world. Nothing seems to be growing. The seemingly "barren" trees of winter have no leaves. No fruit. No beauty. They appear stripped of all life. But don't be fooled...the lack of progress is only what we see. Beneath the snow, life is happening. Growth. Strengthening. A preparation for the bounty to come!

While spring and summer are times of upward growth, winter is a time of downward growth for trees. Instead of their branches spreading up and out and filling with visible life, their roots are growing strong and deep.

Without this season of resting, strengthening, and deepening, the tree wouldn't be able to hold all the blessings God will heap upon its branches in the spring! It would fall over in the first hard wind. In the same way, an immature root system will keep you from being a strong Christian, able to be the hands and voice of Christ in this world—to be a blessing, even as you are blessed by your Father in Heaven.

As Believers, we tend to pray for relief from the winter seasons of life, instead of seeing how deep roots are part of God's plan. We need our roots to grow deep in Christ, because it takes deep, strong roots to bear bigger and more fruit for God's Kingdom.

My friend, if you are experiencing a winter season in your physical or spiritual health…your finances…or your marriage or family, rest assured…

Your world may be shaking.
But God cannot be shaken.

And in these dark days of winter, He is lovingly stretching your roots—deepening you and preparing you for your created purpose. Instead of focusing on your circumstances, I urge you to…

- Focus on the Lord
- Worship Him
- Talk to Him
- Read His Word
- Listen to Him

Really get to know the One who wants nothing more—or less—than all of you. The more difficult the winter season, the deeper your roots can grow. These times of trial are the refining fire He uses to grow your faith and show you how to lean on Him.

Defy the Devil's D's

All too often, we don't see the good of winter. The devil comes to *"steal, kill, and destroy"* (John 10:10)…and he will use this season to sow his…

- **D**oubt and **D**isbelief in your mind
- **D**epression and **D**iscouragement in your heart
- **D**efeat and **D**estruction in your Harvest

And without the joy of spring right in front of us, we can be vulnerable to these attacks…unless we realize that the winter seasons of life are an important part of God's perfect plan. He allows winter to come. If you focus on your problems, the devil will try to use your circumstances to defeat you. Instead, look to God and remember His faithfulness, even when it's hard to see signs of it with your natural eyes. Let the words of this Scripture verse comfort and strengthen you:

> *Therefore the LORD will wait, that He may be gracious to you; and therefore He will be exalted, that He may have mercy on you...Blessed are all those who wait for Him...you shall weep no more. He will be very gracious to you at the sound of your cry; when He hears it, He will answer you...then He will give the rain for your seed with which you sow the ground, and bread of the increase of the earth* (Isaiah 30:18–23).

So wait on the Lord. If you are in a winter season in your life, and you can't seem to feel His Presence...if the future seems uncertain...if you're still waiting to Reap your Harvest...know that God hasn't forgotten you, and He hasn't forgotten your Uncommon Seed or your Uncommon Harvest.

These times of trial are the refining fire He uses to grow your faith and show you how to lean on Him.

He is growing you up to be strong in faith, strong in grace, and strong in the knowledge that He is in control of your life. Know that it is often in our hardest winters that He holds us close and shows us *"the width and length and depth and height"* of His love (Ephesians 3:18).

Your New Beginning Is Coming!

Just as surely as winter comes, spring will follow. You WILL understand His grace and mercy. You WILL see His faithfulness as you walk in an obedient Covenant Relationship with Him! You WILL have a New Beginning in Him and Reap His Uncommon Harvests in your life!

If you're experiencing a "winter" in your physical or spiritual health, your finances, or your relationships, then do this:

- ❧ Water your Seed with prayer, worship, and the Word.
- ❧ Be steadfast and unmovable.
- ❧ Press on toward your high calling in Christ Jesus.
- ❧ Lay aside every weight holding you back.
- ❧ Do *not* give up when you don't see your Harvest!

Spring is just around the corner, a spring of greater vision and a spring of answers to prayer. The more difficult the winter season, the deeper your roots will grow, and the greater your coming Harvest will be.

And because of the winter season, a whole New Beginning can be yours…new joy, new peace, and a new level of contentment in your life in God. Just patiently wait and give your Uncommon Seed time to produce the Uncommon Harvest you're expecting.

Waiting may be painful, but it's the season between Sowing and Reaping. Don't get discouraged if you can't see immediate results. Harvests don't spring up overnight in the natural world, and they don't spring up overnight in the spiritual world either.

Continue trusting in Him.
Continue crying out to Him.
Continue believing Him, because…

He is working ALL things together for your good (Romans 8:28). God IS faithful. Your Uncommon Harvest IS coming!

Here Is Your 10ᵗʰ Harvest Key:

WAIT PATIENTLY FOR YOUR UNCOMMON HARVEST...IT'S COMING!

Let me pray for you...

Heavenly Father, thank You for Your Covenant with us that Seedtime and Harvest shall not cease. We're grateful for Your promise that we WILL Reap Your Uncommon Harvests if we do not lose heart. I ask You to please strengthen Your child's heart as they wait for their Uncommon Seeds to bear fruit. Let Your grace, mercy, strength, peace, and joy guard and protect their body, soul, and spirit while they wait. May they be strong in You and in Your power in the winter season. We thank You in advance for the Harvest Blessing and the New Beginning You have in store for them. I pray this is Jesus' Name. Amen.

Now be encouraged by this testimony of how God blessed Patti, who Sowed Uncommon Seeds into God's Kingdom and waited patiently until she Reaped His Uncommon Harvests for her son John!

'Miracles Do Happen!'

"About three months ago, I Sowed a substantial Seed into Inspiration Ministries with a request for steadfast prayers for my son John. Because of severe depression and suicidal thoughts, he had lost his job of many years and most of his friends, and he almost lost his wife. He was in terrible physical shape and overweight, due

Miracles do happen! My son is now a new man.

to not getting proper nutrition, rest, or exercise. In addition, his teeth were rotten and falling out. He would isolate himself in his dark home and refuse to answer the phone.

"I was heartbroken over my son's condition, and I often lost all contact with him. But things came to a head when he sought help and was hospitalized.

"Thank God John entered a publicly funded psychiatric hospital, where he was diagnosed as having bipolar disorder, along with having some substance abuse challenges. That's when I found out where he was. For the next three days, I traveled about 25 miles to see him until he was discharged. Would he stay on his meds, go to his support group, and keep in contact with me? I knew this was the moment of truth. That's when I called to Sow my Seed and request prayer for God to intervene in my son's life.

"Miracles do happen! My son is now a new man. He got his former job back, and he has worked out every day, losing more than 26 pounds. He has a beautiful smile with new teeth. He keeps his doctor appointments, takes his medications faithfully, and has made new friends. And he is no longer using drugs. He is such a happy, grateful person now.

"The best gift to me is that even though I live 55 miles away, he comes to visit me every Saturday. Before all this happened, he visited my home about four times in four and a half years. Now we have so much fun together. Praise the Lord!" — **Patti**

My friend, what God has done for Patti, He can do for *you!*

BLESSED

...Choose for

yourselves

this day

whom you

will serve...

JOSHUA 24:15b

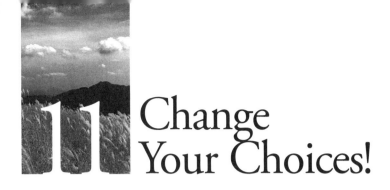

11 Change Your Choices!

Are you tired of your circumstances? Are you frustrated by your inability to break free in some area of your life? Do you wish things could be different?

The truth of the matter is that what we tolerate—whatever we feel too tired, too overwhelmed, or too afraid to do something about—we will not change.

On the other hand, what we refuse to tolerate—what we are willing to confront, we CAN change. How we choose to react to our situation makes a difference. We are the sum total of our choices—both good and bad. The decisions we make today impact everything about tomorrow.

God has given us the awesome, life-changing power of choice. Every day, we can choose between God's plans or the devil's; action or inaction; productivity or laziness; faith or fear; wisdom or foolishness; obedience or sin. Years ago I heard these compelling words:

If you want to change your future, change your choices!

And the choices we make now not only affect our future on

earth: They determine where—and how—we will spend eternity. Your decisions create your circumstances.

But sadly, too many of us are unwilling to make the choices and changes necessary to move forward in God's destiny for our lives. Even though we may complain that we want things to be different, we refuse to move beyond what is familiar to the blessing-filled future He has planned for us.

But this doesn't have to be true of YOU! Even the little changes and seemingly small choices you make can bring huge rewards.

The Life-Changing Power of Choice

Daniel "Rudy" Ruettiger is one who made positive choices that brought powerful changes. One of 14 children in a working-class family, Rudy had no economic advantages.

Nor did he have any special athletic ability or size, at 5' 7" and 165 pounds—nothing that would seem to make his dream of playing football for Notre Dame even remotely realistic.

But the ability to choose is powerful.

Rudy **chose** to begin at Holy Cross College…despite academic and financial obstacles. He **chose** to keep applying to Notre Dame, in spite of multiple rejections. He **chose** to keep praying and working out, to study hard.

And when he finally was accepted for admission, Rudy **chose** to walk on to the scout team and give it his best…even though he didn't get to play.

In the last game of his senior year, Rudy's lifelong dream became reality: He played for Notre Dame. After two plays and one tackle, he was carried off the field on his teammates' shoulders—one of only two players in Notre Dame football history to have been honored this way. And all of his younger brothers after him went on to attend college.

Rudy's **choices** were a life-changing source of inspiration and motivation for his team, coaches, and family. And like him, the power to change your circumstances is in YOUR hands. Your past decisions have created your current circumstances, and your current decisions will create your future circumstances.

> The choices we make now not only affect our future on earth: They determine where—and how—we will spend eternity.

In Luke 13, Jesus tells a story about another young man, but unlike Rudy, this one chose poorly—and reaped what he'd sown. It's the Parable of the Prodigal Son.

This young man was tired of doing the right thing, of working, of being told what to do. He asked for his inheritance, then went off into the world, where he *"squandered his estate with loose living"* (Luke 15:13 NASB). After the money was gone, he discovered that none of his so-called friends were interested in him—and that because of his choices, he was left with nobody who truly cared for him. He was left starving.

Most of us know what happened next—he returned home to ask his father to hire him as a worker. His father, mirroring the love of our Heavenly Father, welcomed his son…and rejoiced.

There was a crucial moment. The son could have kept on

making the same bad choices...kept complaining about his circumstances and the way his former friends were treating him. But if he had made that choice, he would have kept on starving.

You Are MORE Than a Conqueror!

King Hezekiah was king over Judah, and he was very ill. In fact, one of God's prophets had informed the king that he was about to die.

Did Hezekiah simply tolerate his death sentence? Did he allow himself to be overcome by fear and passively accept death as his fate and God's will? No! Hezekiah wanted his situation to change...he wanted to LIVE.

Your past decisions have created your current circumstances, and your current decisions will create your future circumstances.

King Hezekiah needed a supernatural harvest. So he Sowed Seeds of humility before the Lord. He Sowed Seeds of bitter tears as he wept with a broken spirit and a contrite heart. He Sowed Seeds of fervent prayer, asking God to remember his faithfulness as he had served both Him and Israel as a loyal king. And God responded!

Because of Hezekiah's Seeds of humility, prayer, and tears, God granted him an additional 15 years of life. (For Hezekiah's story, see 2 Kings 20.)

Like King Hezekiah, you can refuse to tolerate whatever is going on in your life that is out of sync with God's plans and purposes for you. Choose to refuse what you've been allowing, and you will see the circumstances in your life begin to change!

As I shared with you in Chapter 9, the enemy's intention is to destroy your God-given destiny: *"The thief does not come except to steal, and to kill, and to destroy"* (John 10:10a).

But the good news for you today is that you do NOT have to tolerate sin, sickness, fear, poverty, or any of the devil's plans for you or your loved ones. GOD'S plan is to give you overflowing life through His Son, Jesus Christ: *"I have come that they may have life, and that they may have it more abundantly!"* (John 10:10b)

The devil wants you to believe you're a victim, doomed to remain in bondage, sick, depressed, and impoverished. But according to God and His Word, you are not a victim! No, you are more than a conqueror through Jesus Christ, who loves you (Romans 8:37–39), and you can decide today to change your circumstances by following these seven steps:

1. **REFUSE** to tolerate what you know is not from God in your life.
2. **REPENT** for any sin that has contributed to your circumstances.
3. **REJECT** the fatigue, stress, or fear preventing you from making needed changes.
4. **RECORD** your specific goals for what needs to change in your life and how, with God's help and power, you are going to change them.
5. **RELY** on Him to replace old, negative habits with new, positive habits.
6. **REQUEST** God's mercy, strength, and courage to obey as you humble yourself before Him.
7. **REAP** His Harvests as you Sow Seeds of your time, talent, and treasure into His Kingdom!

Because of who you are, you don't have to think, act, or respond to life's circumstances as though you were a helpless victim of other people's choices. You can begin today to make the kind of choices that a conqueror makes!

We Reap What We Sow

Keep in mind that your decisions—both big and small—schedule the seasons of your life. The Uncommon Seeds you Sow now will determine what you will Reap during those seasons. If you don't like the Harvests you're Reaping, then change the Seed you're Sowing!

When we choose to walk in obedience to God and His Word, He will heap blessing after blessing upon us.

If you want to consistently Reap the things of the Spirit, then make sure you are consistently Sowing Seeds according to the Spirit. God makes it very clear: When we walk in disobedience, we will Reap some very unpleasant Harvests. (See Deuteronomy 28:15–68.)

However, when we choose to walk in obedience to God and His Word, He will heap blessing after blessing upon us (See Deuteronomy 28:1–14.) He loves us so much, and His heart's desire is that we love Him and choose to live in an unending Covenant Relationship with Him:

> *I call heaven and earth as witnesses today against you, that I have set before you life and death, blessing and cursing; therefore* **choose life,** *that both you and your descendants may live; that you may love the LORD your God, that you may obey His voice, and that you may cling to Him, for He is your life and the length of your days; and that you may dwell in the land which the LORD*

swore to your fathers, to Abraham, Isaac, and Jacob, to give them (Deuteronomy 30:19–20).

To continually Reap God's Uncommon Harvests in your life, not only must you obediently Sow Uncommon Seeds into Good Ground, but you must continually choose to Sow Seeds of worship, prayer, and faithful obedience to God's Word. Cling to Him, for He is your life!

Here Is Your 11th Harvest Key:
YOUR DECISIONS CREATE YOUR CIRCUMSTANCES!

Let me pray for you…

Heavenly Father, we praise You for giving us the power of choice. Thank you that we are not victims, but we are more than conquerors through Your Son, who loves us. I pray for Your child, that You would lead them into Your truth. Reveal to them any poor choices they have made that are impacting their current circumstances so they can repent. Give them the desire to seek Your wisdom for every choice they need to make to bring about the changes needed in their circumstances. I pray this in Jesus' Name. Amen.

Now be encouraged by this testimony of how God blessed Benitee, who Sowed small Uncommon Seeds into God's Kingdom and Reaped great Uncommon Harvests from Him!

'I Was Behind Two Months on My Mortgage'

"Several months ago, I suddenly became a single parent, was laid off from my job of nearly seven years, and suffered a serious

I continued to trust God to faithfully provide me with the breakthroughs I needed.

illness. As a result of these troublesome circumstances, I was behind two months on my mortgage and utilities, and I was using a credit card to pay for living expenses.

"Nevertheless, I continued to trust God to faithfully provide me with the breakthroughs I needed. Even during this time of financial difficulty, I continued Sowing my financial Seeds into God's Kingdom through Inspiration Ministries.

"This was a period when gas prices were soaring, and the child-care costs for my two small daughters had increased significantly. But God was faithful to bless us and meet our needs. We always had food on our table and clothes to wear, our utilities were never turned off, and after I regained my health, the Lord blessed me with a new job!

"Now I've received an unexpected windfall of over $7,000 that will allow me to bring my mortgage up to date, pay my property taxes, and get my credit card balance to zero. I thank God for these miraculous breakthroughs!"

— Benitee

My friend, what God has done for Benitee, He can do for *you!*

BLESSED

He who sows sparingly will also reap sparingly, and he who sows bountifully will also reap bountifully. So let each one give as he purposes in his heart, not grudgingly or of necessity; for God loves a cheerful giver.

2 CORINTHIANS 9:6–7

12 Continuous Sowing, Continuous Reaping!

One of the most important lessons I've learned about Sowing and Reaping is that there are three things God expects me to do if I want to Reap His Harvest of Blessings from the Seeds I have Sown into His Kingdom:

* Exercise My Faith
* Obey Him
* Expect a Harvest

Experience has taught Barbara and me over and over again that as we faithfully and obediently Sow Seeds wherever, whenever, and however God directs, we can expect to consistently Reap His Harvests in our lives. Why?

Because God is ALWAYS faithful to His Word!

In Genesis 8:22, God promised, *"While the earth remains, seedtime and harvest...**shall not cease**."* His Seedtime and Harvest principle will never end...it is an ETERNAL principle. He has **promised** that when we Sow, we WILL Reap!

A Hundredfold Harvest

Isaac is just one of the many Biblical examples of how obedience, faithfulness, and Seed Sowing result in God's tremendous Harvest blessings:

> *There was a famine in the land... Then the LORD appeared to him [Isaac] and said: "Do not go down to Egypt; live in the land of which I shall tell you. Dwell in this land, and I will be with you and bless you; for to you and your descendants I give all these lands, and I will perform the oath which I swore to Abraham your father...* **Then Isaac sowed in that land, and reaped in the same year a hundredfold; and the LORD blessed him. The man began to prosper, and continued prospering until he became very prosperous** (Genesis 26:1–14).

During a time of famine, God told Isaac not to go down to Egypt, where he would have had plenty of food and water for his household. Instead, he was to remain in the land God had promised to his father Abraham.

When we read a reference to Egypt in the Bible, it refers not only to a physical, geographical location, but also has a spiritual parallel to the world's system and way of doing things. God was commanding Isaac, "Don't look to the world or to natural things to provide for you during this time of famine. Look to *Me!*"

Imagine what it meant for Isaac to stay where there was a *"famine in the land"*... terrible thirst...starvation...extreme lack... dire need...barren wasteland. It was in the midst of a desperate situation like this that God told Isaac to remain in the Promised

Land. With a future that looked so bleak, Isaac could have been tempted to doubt God's love and provision.

I wonder if perhaps in response to God's command to remain in that place of famine, Isaac remembered when he was a boy and his father Abraham had taken him up to the mountain. Maybe he recalled the terrible moment when his dad had tied him to the altar in obedience to God as he struggled with what seemed like the death of his son and God's Covenant Promise to him.

Don't look to the world... look to Me!

Perhaps the thought of staying in a place where people where dying of thirst and starvation would have caused Isaac to experience anew the fear and confusion he had felt as he lay there trembling while the man who loved him more than his own life raised his arm to sacrifice the son who was his promised seed. And then I wonder if Isaac would have remembered hearing the rustling of leaves in the bush and the bleating of the ram that God had provided once Abraham had proven to himself and the Lord that he was willing to obey at any cost.

And Isaac's faith in God's faithfulness and love—even in the midst of what looked like a desperately hopeless situation—would have risen within him, giving him the courage to obey God and wait with expectant hopefulness for His blessing, even in the midst of that famine. He knew his source was God, and God alone. So what did Isaac do?

Isaac Sowed Seeds!

Keep in mind that in a time of famine, seeds are precious. They are the only hope for a future harvest. No one...no one... plants seeds when there's no water, because seeds CANNOT grow without it. But Isaac sowed seeds in the middle of a terrible drought. And what were the results? Read these verses again:

> Then Isaac sowed in that land, **and reaped in the same year a hundredfold; and the LORD blessed him** (v. 12).

In response to his obedience, faith, and Seed Sowing, Isaac received a "*hundredfold*" harvest! What a powerful example of how to release God's Covenant Blessings in our lives.

Continuous Sowing Brings Continuous Harvests!

I don't know what kind of "famine" you may be experiencing in your life today. But I do know you have a choice.

You can look to yourself…the world…your job…your family…your friends…your church…or your government to be the source of your supply, or you can exercise your faith, obey God, Sow an Uncommon Seed…and then wait with expectancy for God to step into the circumstances of your life with His Uncommon Harvest of Blessings!

Continuous Sowing Brings Continuous Harvests!

Every farmer knows if he wants to reap a continuous harvest, he must continually sow seeds. This cycle of Sowing and Reaping must be maintained, both in the natural AND in the spiritual.

But the opposite is also true: Irregular Sowing results in irregular Harvests. And no Sowing results in no Harvests. Sowing isn't a one-time thing…and *neither is Reaping*. God can do amazing things for you and through you when you're surrendered to Him!

A life filled with God's Uncommon Harvests is one that is filled with Sowing Uncommon Seeds. Your time, talent, and treasure, along with praise, prayer, and obedience— all are Seeds you can Sow to honor God and Reap the Harvests He has in store for you. In this way, He will bless you and make you a blessing.

Sowing isn't a one-time thing... and neither is Reaping.

We must develop the habit of continuously Sowing—even in times of famine.... especially in times of famine...so that we can live in the habit of continuously Reaping. The Seeds you Sow today will decide tomorrow's Harvests. When you determine in your heart to be a faithful Sower, even in times of famine, God will not allow you to run out of Seed:

> *"Now may He who supplies seed to the sower,*
> *and bread for food, supply and multiply the seed you*
> *have sown and increase the fruits of your righteousness"*
> (2 Corinthians 9:10).

However, His Harvest of Blessings only come as a result of our faith-filled obedience to Him. God wants you to…

❦ **Act in Faith!**
❦ **Obey Him!**
❦ **Expect Your Harvest!**

Your Heavenly Father loves you and wants to…

❦ **Meet your needs!**
❦ **Bless you with His Uncommon Harvests!**

My Challenge for You

When you are faithful to Sow an Uncommon Seed, God is faithful to release His Uncommon Harvests. When you release the Seed in your hands, God releases the Harvests in His hands.

Some people are afraid to Sow their Seed because they fear that once their Seed has left their hand, it has left their life. This couldn't be further from the truth. Your Seed never leaves your life! God receives it and multiplies it back into your life in the form of a Harvest so that you are blessed, you can bless others, and He is glorified!

Your Seed never leaves your life! God receives it and multiplies it back!

Perhaps you're a Believer who has Sown Seeds sporadically—or maybe not at all—because you're experiencing a season of famine in your life. If so, I challenge you today to take a step of faith. Obey God. Continually Sow your Uncommon Seeds into Good Ground, and then wait on Him for His Uncommon Harvests, because they will surely come. Yes, even in a time of famine!

Here Is Your 12ᵗʰ Harvest Key:

CONTINUOUS SOWING RESULTS IN CONTINUOUS REAPING!

Let me pray for you…

Heavenly Father, thank You for Your deep and abiding love for us. We're grateful for all of the Harvest Blessings You want to pour out on our lives as we respond to You with faith, obedience, and expectancy. I ask You to please water the Seeds that have been planted in the heart and mind of Your child as they have read this book. Cause Your eternal Covenant of Seedtime and Harvest to be a guiding truth by which they live. May they be blessed, and may they be a blessing as they continually Sow Seeds and continually Reap Your Harvests all the days of their life. I pray this in Jesus' Name. Amen.

Now be encouraged by this testimony of how God blessed David and Valerie, who continually Sowed their Uncommon Seeds into God's Kingdom and continually Reaped their Uncommon Harvests from Him!

'The Uncommon Harvests Keep Getting Better!'

David and Valerie were experiencing a season of personal challenge. Their years of labor in the service of Jesus Christ had brought many Souls into God's Kingdom, and they were feeling led by the Holy Spirit to take an exciting new leap of faith.

Their small apartment had served them well enough, but they began believing God for something better for their family. So they Sowed their first $58 Seed into the Good Ground of Inspiration Ministries.

"We soon found ourselves living in a home that was beyond our wildest dreams! We have the three bedrooms we need, a winding staircase, fireplace, basement, two-car garage, and even a sunroom! We know now that God had an even better home for us than we had imagined! We couldn't be happier!"

This was only the beginning of David and Valerie's Uncommon Harvests. A few months later, they purchased an investment home to remodel and then resell for a substantial profit. "Amazingly, we went from being apartment dwellers to owning two homes in only six months!"

And the blessings continued. Their son had some academic challenges, and they were told it would be months before he could enter the program he needed. But as they continued to trust God and faithfully Sow their Uncommon Seeds, David and Valerie soon were told that their son's application had been moved to the front of the line! Little David is now getting the education he needs!

We see how God has guided every step we've taken since we began Sowing our Uncommon Seed into Inspiration Ministries.

In addition, David and Valerie share a call to pastor, and they have started a new church, which is growing as David preaches and Valerie ministers in both the Word and music.

What have they learned during this wonderful time of reaping God's Harvest of Blessings?

"We see how God has guided every step we've taken since we began Sowing our Uncommon Seed into Inspiration Ministries. In less than a year, we have begun living in our dream home, seen our child's needs met, bought an investment home, and started a wonderful ministry in an area where the people needed it the most. We know our partnership with you is giving the truth of the Gospel to millions of people around the world." — David & Valerie

My friend, what God has done for David and Valerie, He can do for *you!*

BLESSED
CONCLUSION

Jump into God's River of Blessing!

Sowing and Reaping, Seedtime and Harvest…this is God's cycle of blessing. He intends for this to be your way of life.

As you faithfully apply the Scriptural principles of this book—exercising your faith, obeying God's Word and the voice of His Holy Spirit, and expecting Him to bless you so that you might be a blessing to others—His Uncommon Harvests will come.

I invite you today to jump into the river of God's blessing! Choose to begin now to experience a life filled with Seedtime and Harvest. Get into His rhythm of giving and receiving, and then giving and receiving again. Walk in a continual, loving, obedient Covenant Relationship with the Lord and make these principles a lifestyle. Live by them. If you do…you will live out of them.

Share your story and encourage our other Inspiration Partners with your testimony of God's goodness!

Is the Holy Spirit stirring your heart to begin Sowing Uncommon Seeds so that He can bless you with His Uncommon Harvests and equip you to be a blessing to others? If so, I invite you to use the coupons I've included in the back of this book to Sow a financial Seed into God's Kingdom through the Good Ground of Inspiration Ministries.

BLESSED
CONCLUSION

Remember…

Faith + Obedience + Expectancy = God's Uncommon Harvests!

We would love to hear *your* testimony of how your Uncommon Seeds result in God's Uncommon Harvests. Please use the contact information on the cover to write, email, or call to encourage us with your personal story of God's faithfulness. When writing, please also include your picture if possible. We will share your story and encourage our other Inspiration Partners with your testimony of God's goodness!

DAVID *and* **BARBARA**, I want to be blessed by God *AND* be a blessing to others. Here is my financial Seed to save SOULS in the nations of the world!

☐ Enclosed is my Seed for Souls of $/£_____.

Name _____

Address _____

_____

Email _____

Phone _____

I am paying by:
☐ Check/Money Order
☐ Credit/Debit Card
(Please fill out information on the reverse side of this form.)

INSP()IRATION
MINISTRIES

PLEASE MAKE CHECK OR MONEY ORDER PAYABLE TO AND RETURN TO:
INSPIRATION MINISTRIES • PO Box 7750 • Charlotte, NC 28241
INSPIRATION MINISTRIES UK • Admail 3905 • London, W1A 1ZT • UK
Registered Charity Number 1119076
www.inspiration.org

DAVID *and* **BARBARA**, I want to be blessed by God *AND* be a blessing to others. Here is my financial Seed to save SOULS in the nations of the world!

☐ Enclosed is my Seed for Souls of $/£_____.

Name _____

Address _____

_____

Email _____

Phone _____

I am paying by:
☐ Check/Money Order
☐ Credit/Debit Card
(Please fill out information on the reverse side of this form.)

INSP()IRATION
MINISTRIES

PLEASE MAKE CHECK OR MONEY ORDER PAYABLE TO AND RETURN TO:
INSPIRATION MINISTRIES • PO Box 7750 • Charlotte, NC 28241
INSPIRATION MINISTRIES UK • Admail 3905 • London, W1A 1ZT • UK
Registered Charity Number 1119076
www.inspiration.org

DAVID *and* **BARBARA**, I want to be blessed by God *AND* be a blessing to others. Here is my financial Seed to save SOULS in the nations of the world!

☐ Enclosed is my Seed for Souls of $/£_____.

Name _____

Address _____

_____

Email _____

Phone _____

I am paying by:
☐ Check/Money Order
☐ Credit/Debit Card
(Please fill out information on the reverse side of this form.)

INSP()IRATION
MINISTRIES

PLEASE MAKE CHECK OR MONEY ORDER PAYABLE TO AND RETURN TO:
INSPIRATION MINISTRIES • PO Box 7750 • Charlotte, NC 28241
INSPIRATION MINISTRIES UK • Admail 3905 • London, W1A 1ZT • UK
Registered Charity Number 1119076
www.inspiration.org

FILL OUT THIS SECTION ONLY IF USING A CREDIT OR DEBIT CARD

$/£_____ Please charge this amount to my:

☐ **VISA** ☐ **MasterCard** ☐ **Discover** ☐ **American Express**
☐ **Maestro** ☐ **Switch** ☐ **VISA Electron** ☐ **Solo**

Card Number ___|___|___|___|___|___|___|___|___|___|___|___|___|___|___|___|___|___

CCV ___ ___ ___ *(3-digit security code on back of card)*

Expiration Date ___ ___ / ___ ___   Start Date ___ ___ / ___ ___   Issue No. ___ ___ / ___ ___
(Maestro, Switch & Solo)   *(Switch only)*

Signature _____

Print Name _____

Phone Number _____

FILL OUT THIS SECTION ONLY IF USING A CREDIT OR DEBIT CARD

$/£_____ Please charge this amount to my:

☐ **VISA** ☐ **MasterCard** ☐ **Discover** ☐ **American Express**
☐ **Maestro** ☐ **Switch** ☐ **VISA Electron** ☐ **Solo**

Card Number ___|___|___|___|___|___|___|___|___|___|___|___|___|___|___|___|___|___

CCV ___ ___ ___ *(3-digit security code on back of card)*

Expiration Date ___ ___ / ___ ___   Start Date ___ ___ / ___ ___   Issue No. ___ ___ / ___ ___
(Maestro, Switch & Solo)   *(Switch only)*

Signature _____

Print Name _____

Phone Number _____

FILL OUT THIS SECTION ONLY IF USING A CREDIT OR DEBIT CARD

$/£_____ Please charge this amount to my:

☐ **VISA** ☐ **MasterCard** ☐ **Discover** ☐ **American Express**
☐ **Maestro** ☐ **Switch** ☐ **VISA Electron** ☐ **Solo**

Card Number ___|___|___|___|___|___|___|___|___|___|___|___|___|___|___|___|___|___

CCV ___ ___ ___ *(3-digit security code on back of card)*

Expiration Date ___ ___ / ___ ___   Start Date ___ ___ / ___ ___   Issue No. ___ ___ / ___ ___
(Maestro, Switch & Solo)   *(Switch only)*

Signature _____

Print Name _____

Phone Number _____

DAVID *and* BARBARA, I want to be blessed by God *AND* be a blessing to others. Here is my financial Seed to save SOULS in the nations of the world!

☐ Enclosed is my Seed for Souls of $/£_____.

Name _____

Address _____

_____

Email _____

Phone _____

I am paying by:
☐ Check/Money Order
☐ Credit/Debit Card
(Please fill out information on the reverse side of this form.)

INSP|RATION
MINISTRIES

PLEASE MAKE CHECK OR
MONEY ORDER PAYABLE
TO AND RETURN TO:
| INSPIRATION MINISTRIES • PO Box 7750 • Charlotte, NC 28241
INSPIRATION MINISTRIES UK • Admail 3905 • London, W1A 1ZT • UK
Registered Charity Number 1119076
www.inspiration.org

DAVID *and* BARBARA, I want to be blessed by God *AND* be a blessing to others. Here is my financial Seed to save SOULS in the nations of the world!

☐ Enclosed is my Seed for Souls of $/£_____.

Name _____

Address _____

_____

Email _____

Phone _____

I am paying by:
☐ Check/Money Order
☐ Credit/Debit Card
(Please fill out information on the reverse side of this form.)

INSP|RATION
MINISTRIES

PLEASE MAKE CHECK OR
MONEY ORDER PAYABLE
TO AND RETURN TO:
| INSPIRATION MINISTRIES • PO Box 7750 • Charlotte, NC 28241
INSPIRATION MINISTRIES UK • Admail 3905 • London, W1A 1ZT • UK
Registered Charity Number 1119076
www.inspiration.org

DAVID *and* BARBARA, I want to be blessed by God *AND* be a blessing to others. Here is my financial Seed to save SOULS in the nations of the world!

☐ Enclosed is my Seed for Souls of $/£_____.

Name _____

Address _____

_____

Email _____

Phone _____

I am paying by:
☐ Check/Money Order
☐ Credit/Debit Card
(Please fill out information on the reverse side of this form.)

INSP|RATION
MINISTRIES

PLEASE MAKE CHECK OR
MONEY ORDER PAYABLE
TO AND RETURN TO:
| INSPIRATION MINISTRIES • PO Box 7750 • Charlotte, NC 28241
INSPIRATION MINISTRIES UK • Admail 3905 • London, W1A 1ZT • UK
Registered Charity Number 1119076
www.inspiration.org

FILL OUT THIS SECTION ONLY IF USING A CREDIT OR DEBIT CARD

$/£_____ Please charge this amount to my:

☐ **VISA** ☐ **MasterCard** ☐ **Discover** ☐ **American Express**
☐ **Maestro** ☐ **Switch** ☐ **VISA Electron** ☐ **Solo**

Card Number __|__|__|__|__|__|__|__|__|__|__|__|__|__|__|__|__|__

CCV ___ ___ ___ *(3-digit security code on back of card)*

Expiration Date ___ ___ / ___ ___   Start Date ___ ___ / ___ ___   Issue No. ___ ___ / ___ ___
(Maestro, Switch & Solo)   *(Switch only)*

Signature _____

Print Name _____

Phone Number _____

....

FILL OUT THIS SECTION ONLY IF USING A CREDIT OR DEBIT CARD

$/£_____ Please charge this amount to my:

☐ **VISA** ☐ **MasterCard** ☐ **Discover** ☐ **American Express**
☐ **Maestro** ☐ **Switch** ☐ **VISA Electron** ☐ **Solo**

Card Number __|__|__|__|__|__|__|__|__|__|__|__|__|__|__|__|__|__

CCV ___ ___ ___ *(3-digit security code on back of card)*

Expiration Date ___ ___ / ___ ___   Start Date ___ ___ / ___ ___   Issue No. ___ ___ / ___ ___
(Maestro, Switch & Solo)   *(Switch only)*

Signature _____

Print Name _____

Phone Number _____

....

FILL OUT THIS SECTION ONLY IF USING A CREDIT OR DEBIT CARD

$/£_____ Please charge this amount to my:

☐ **VISA** ☐ **MasterCard** ☐ **Discover** ☐ **American Express**
☐ **Maestro** ☐ **Switch** ☐ **VISA Electron** ☐ **Solo**

Card Number __|__|__|__|__|__|__|__|__|__|__|__|__|__|__|__|__|__

CCV ___ ___ ___ *(3-digit security code on back of card)*

Expiration Date ___ ___ / ___ ___   Start Date ___ ___ / ___ ___   Issue No. ___ ___ / ___ ___
(Maestro, Switch & Solo)   *(Switch only)*

Signature _____

Print Name _____

Phone Number _____

DAVID CERULLO has a vision to impact people for Christ worldwide through media and has combined his strong business skills with his passion for ministry to fulfill his God-given mission.

He has established *INSPIRATION MINISTRIES*, an international media ministry based at the City of Light in South Carolina, that reaches out to more than 1.2 billion Souls in over 120 nations with the Gospel of Jesus Christ through three different television networks.

Having achieved national and international recognition as a television broadcaster and religious leader, David is a member of the National Cable Television Association, the Cable and Telecommunications Association for Marketing, the National Association of Television Program Executives, and has served on the Board of Directors for the National Religious Broadcasters Association.

David and his wife, Barbara, host a popular daily television program, *"INSPIRATION TODAY!"* They have been married for more than 36 years and have two adult children and five grandchildren.

Visit their website at **www.inspiration.org** to receive teaching from the Word, ministry updates, or to request prayer.

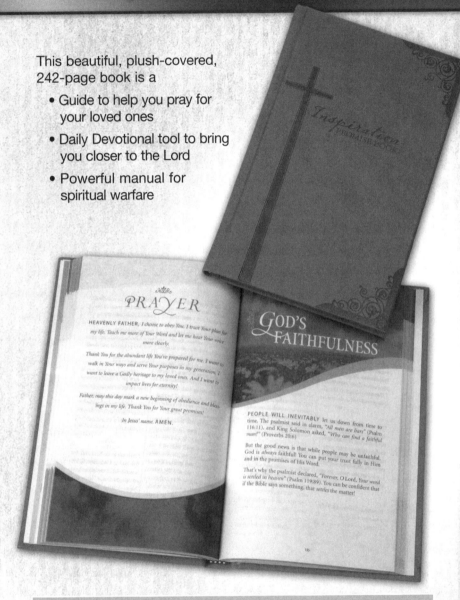

God Answers Prayer!

"If two of you agree on earth concerning anything that they ask, it will be done for them by My Father in Heaven."
— MATTHEW 18:19

"Thanks so much for your prayers for my husband Michael, who had been diagnosed with cancer. Michael went back for a check-up, and the doctor said his cancer is GONE! Praise the Lord!" — HELEN

"Your prayers and those of our friends have brought Divine healing to my mom's thyroid disease! She's returned to her former health!" — JAMES

"My wife's back was healed when your prayer minister agreed with me in prayer!" — ALLEN

"Thank you for your prayers! I've received a total healing regarding high blood pressure and a possible stroke." — IBIRONKE

Our prayer ministers welcome the opportunity to agree together with you in prayer and believe God to step into the circumstances of your life with His supernatural power!

**In the U.S., call 803-578-1800 7 days a week, 24 hours a day.
In the U.K., call 0845 683 0584 Monday – Friday, 09:30 – 21:30.
Or email your prayer request to Prayer@inspiration.org.**

"Thank you for having one of your Prayer Ministers call and pray with me today. The call came at just the right time, and it made me feel like someone really cares. Again, thank you for the call just to pray with me." — GLORIA

Do You Need a MIRACLE from God?

God is a God of MIRACLES!

Do you need God's supernatural intervention today in your...

- **BODY, SOUL, OR SPIRIT?**
- **FINANCES, HOME, OR JOB?**
- **RELATIONSHIPS WITH LOVED ONES?**

This life-changing ministry resource will help you experience the miracle you need from Him!

Get ready to receive YOUR miracle!

"How to Receive Your Miracle tells me how to look forward to God's promises for complete healing in my life. This book has been an eye opener for me to the keys of living!" — KAREN

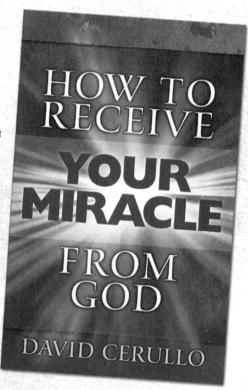

HOW TO RECEIVE YOUR MIRACLE FROM GOD

DAVID CERULLO

HOPE FOR *Your* NEW BEGINNING

God wants to step into the circumstances of your life with His supernatural breakthroughs!

If you need a New Beginning in your...

Marriage • Job
Health • Finances
Children

...Hope For Your New Beginning book and audio CD will provide the tools you need to experience victory and abundance in Christ.

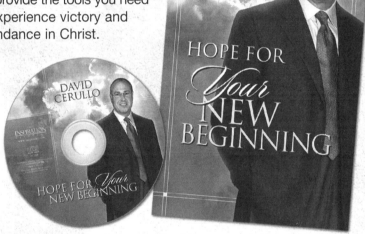

DAVID CERULLO

HOPE FOR *Your* NEW BEGINNING

DAVID CERULLO

HOPE FOR *Your* NEW BEGINNING

*"I was blessed by your book **New Beginnings**. This is such a profound word from the heart of God, and I have asked the Lord to order my steps into His New Beginning. I want all the miracles and new beginnings He has ordained for my life and for my family's life this year and for years to come."* — INGRID

Sow a Seed for Souls and receive one or more of these with us to impact people for Christ worldwide!

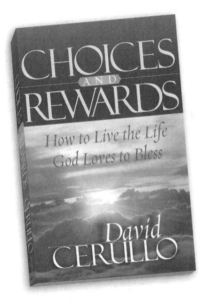

GOD'S ANSWERS
FOR YOUR TIMES OF TROUBLE

Find a **REST**-filled Life in a **STRESS**-filled World!

GOD'S ANSWERS FOR YOUR TIMES OF TROUBLE WILL GIVE YOU POWERFUL KEYS FOR LIVING IN THE PEACE AND PROSPERITY OF GOD!

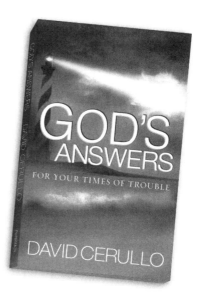

You'll learn how to...

- **GAIN** Victory in your family, health, and finances

- **GRASP** God's provision for your every need

- **CONQUER** the spirit of fear

- **MOVE** from fretting to faith

"God's Answers for Your Times of Trouble is the best thing that has ever happened to me. I was at an all time low when I received it, but it has changed my life. Thank you for saving my life!" — ALFRED

Sow a Seed for Souls and receive one or more of these with us to impact people for Christ worldwide!

Are YOU

"BATTLE FOR YOUR LIFE" VICTORY PACK
Will Give You the Tools You Need to Triumph Over the Enemy!

This powerful array of spiritual resources includes:

- *Battle for Your Life.* This timely manual will equip you to pull down enemy strongholds so you can discover God's destiny for your life!

- **Three video DVDs** of a teaching series on spiritual warfare. You'll want to watch the DVDs with your family, small group, or Sunday school class.

- **The audio CDs** of messages are a wonderful resource to listen to in your car, helping you put on the *"full armor of God"* each day!

- **A bookmark** to remind you of key Biblical principles for gaining victory over Satan. Keep it in your Bible or in your copy of the *Battle for Your Life* book!

Ready for **BATTLE?**

Don't Be Unprotected!

Use the Weapons God Has Given You to Win This Spiritual War!

The war is real. The enemy is real. His power is real. His agenda to steal, kill, and destroy is real.

You don't need to be a victim!

The resources in the **"BATTLE FOR YOUR LIFE"** VICTORY PACK will place in your hands the vital keys you need for victorious spiritual warfare in your life.

"I have read your book Battle for Your Life, and I see now where Satan has almost destroyed me and my family. But I'm fighting back now that I realize a real spiritual evil is assaulting my children and me and my job. Thanks and God bless you!" — HUGH

INSPIRATION *Today!*

with David and Barbara Cerullo

We Are Here for *You*

...Bringing You God's Encouragement, Inspiration, and Hope!

Visit our website at www.inspiration.org for "Inspiration Today!" air dates and times.

INSPIRATION

Blessed to Be a Blessing

Devotional Magazine

You'll love the daily devotionals, testimonies, and personal messages from David and Barbara Cerullo.

"Your monthly devotional magazine helps us get through the day. Our family has much adversity coming at us to steal our faith, but the devotional helps us keep trusting in God." — BILL & SUSAN